Enhance your enjoyment of
*Physics, Dance, and the Pas de Deux*
by Kenneth Laws and Cynthia Harvey
with
*PHYSICS, DANCE, AND THE PAS DE DEUX:
SPECIAL INSTRUCTIONAL VIDEO*
0 02 871327 3     $35.00

Designed and produced specifically to accompany the book *Physics, Dance, and the Pas de Deux,* this 30-minute videotape presentation illustrates the principles of physics as applied to dance and to partnering. The video includes dance movements specially performed by Julie Kent and Benjamin Pierce of American Ballet Theatre, along with a well-known example from the repertoire—the "Black Swan" *pas de deux* from *Swan Lake,* as danced by Evelyn Hart, Peter Shauffuss, and the London Festival Ballet. Kenneth Laws and Cynthia Harvey narrate the videotape, explaining how each dance segment demonstrates the rules of physics in action. Slow-motion replays and special graphics help to make the ideas of physics and the workings of dance readily understandable.

*To order by check or credit card, or for more information, please write to Macmillan Publishing Company, 100 Front Street, Riverside, NJ 08075.*

*Physics, Dance, and the
Pas de Deux*

# Physics, Dance, and the Pas de Deux

KENNETH LAWS
CYNTHIA HARVEY

Photographs by MARTHA SWOPE

Foreword by KEVIN McKENZIE

SCHIRMER BOOKS
*An Imprint of Macmillan Publishing Company*
NEW YORK

Maxwell Macmillan Canada
TORONTO

Maxwell Macmillan International
NEW YORK   OXFORD   SINGAPORE   SYDNEY

Coventry University

Schirmer Books
An Imprint of Macmillan Publishing Company
866 Third Avenue, New York, N.Y. 10022

Maxwell Macmillan Canada, Inc.
1200 Eglinton Avenue East, Suite 200
Don Mills, Ontario M3C 3N1

Macmillan, Inc., is part of the Maxwell
Communication Group of Companies.

Library of Congress Catalog Card Number: 93-39903

**Printed in the United States of America**

printing number

1   2   3   4   5   6   7   8   9   10

---

**Library of Congress Cataloging-in-Publication Data**

Laws, Kenneth.
    Physics, dance, and the pas de deux / Kenneth Laws and Cynthia
Harvey ; photographs by Martha Swope.
        p.      cm.
    Includes bibliographical references and index.
    ISBN 0-02-871326-5
    1. Ballet dancing—Pas de deux—Physiological aspects.   2. Human
mechanics.   3. Kinesiology.   4. Biophysics.   I. Harvey, Cynthia.
II. Title.
QP310.D35L389   1994
612'.04—dc20                                              93-39903
                                                          CIP

---

The paper used in this publication meets the minimum requirements of American National
Standard for Information Sciences–Permanence of Paper for Printed Library Materials.
ANSI Z3948-1984. ∞ ™

# Contents

*Contents*

*viii*

# Foreword

Upon first glancing at this book, I thought, "Oh, no! Someone is trying to make a science of art!" But upon further reading, I realized that here is a subject that can bring the intimidating factor of "dance as illusion" to a manageable level. Many times I have found that there is a portion of the audience that loves dance, but the mystery of the art form leaves them not knowing how to talk about or how to relate to what they have just seen.

The objective of dance is to move one on an emotional and visceral level—in short, to speak to one. However, it *is* a physical form, and Kenneth Laws and Cynthia Harvey have managed to explain how dance works physically without confusing the issue of what is special about the dance. The laws of physics are illuminated by the artists without compromising the aesthetics of the art. Here we can understand how that is done.

Kevin McKenzie
*Artistic Director*
*American Ballet Theatre*

# *Preface*

This book is the result of a collaboration between a professional dancer and a physicist, not the most likely of alliances! One of us is a principal dancer in one of the best-known ballet companies in the world, and brings many years of dance experience to the collaboration. As a dancer particularly adept at analyzing what she is doing with her craft, she has the interest and motivation to share that approach with others. The other half of the team is a physicist with seventeen years of ballet experience on an av-ocational level, who has an unusual approach to dance. His experience in dance didn't begin until after fifteen years of teaching college-level physics, so the inclination to analyze movement in physical terms was almost automatic from the beginning of that dance activity.

The book *The Physics of Dance*,[1] published in 1984, was a solo journey by a physicist/amateur dancer. That work estab-lished the viability and usefulness of physics as applied to dance movement. This follow-up book evolved for several reasons. First, an additional ten years of thinking, talking, and writing about the physics of dance has given the physicist/author many additional insights. Second, it became increasingly clear that a "real" dancer would add insights that were unique. Third, both authors feel that the *pas de deux* is the epitome of dance—the highest, most challenging, and most beautiful aspect of dance, therefore deserving of deeper analysis than that appearing in *The Physics of Dance*. Finally, since dance is a dynamic visual art form that cannot be fully portrayed by static photography, and considering the widespread use of video cassettes, we had the opportunity to include a video cassette as a part of this book.

Co-authors Cynthia Harvey and Kenneth Laws consult during
the photography session for the book.

Our collaboration began in 1990. Company touring schedules
created a logistical nightmare as we tried to find ways to discuss
all we wanted to discuss. There were memorable times when we
argued in a New York apartment about whether a dancer could
begin a partnered turn from an off-axis force without being off
balance at the beginning of the turn, or where the supporting
force had to be when a dancer is supported in a particular lift.
We often wrestled with terminology; dancers sometimes have
different meanings for words that physicists use automatically
without realizing the assumptions they are making. But through
this exhilarating process, we did eventually come to agreement,
and both found ourselves adjusting the way we articulated our
understandings. We hope some of the flavor of our wrestling
with ideas is evident in this book.

We have strengthened our belief that this approach is not only
intriguing, but that it is also useful for both dancers and observers of dance. In the ten years since *The Physics of Dance* was
published, the number of dance aficionados who are willing to
think physically about this art form has increased dramatically. It
is no longer so unusual to find dance teachers explaining how

forces act on the body from the floor, or how to adjust the location of the body's center of gravity in order to accomplish some movement. And it is not unusual to find scientists who enjoy the fact that science *can* speak usefully to the arts. There *is* a role for physicists wishing to contribute something useful to artists or observers of the arts, and a role for dancers who can communicate a deeper sense of how they dance.

There are others—kinesiologists, dance therapists, physical therapists, physicians in sports medicine or dance medicine, and dance critics or writers—who can benefit by the deeper understanding of movement exemplified by this approach. Even students of physics may be intrigued by this application of their field of study to a readily observable phenomenon.

Many persons have helped us in this project. The Central Pennsylvania Youth Ballet has been the training ground for a physicist captured by the beauty of dance. Marcia Dale Weary, the artistic director of that wonderful school, and Richard Cook, its associate artistic director, have been the source of most of this physicist's understanding of ballet. Valuable input has been contributed by some who are neither dancers nor scientists, and who have tried to prevent us from becoming too engrossed in our own technical ways of expressing ideas—Chris Murphy (Cynthia's husband), Peggy Garrett (English professor and balletomane from Dickinson College), Diane Brancazio (ice skater/engineer from Boston), Paul Harvath ("Photos on Ice"), and many others. Maribeth Payne, editor for *The Physics of Dance*, continued to provide cooperation and support for this book. Dickinson College has provided funds, space, and other, less tangible support for the project.

## The Artists

Many of the photographs appearing in this book are taken from the earlier *The Physics of Dance*. Two dancers—Lisa de Ribère and Sean Lavery—spent a long and exhausting day in the summer of 1983 performing for the photographer the movements analyzed in the book.

Lisa is a native of York, Pennsylvania, and received early training at the Central Pennsylvania Youth Ballet and at the school of the Pennsylvania Ballet. After three years at the School of American Ballet she joined George Balanchine's New York City Ballet at the age of 16. She danced and toured extensively with that

Lisa de Ribère and Sean Lavery, the two artists who danced the movements appearing in *The Physics of Dance*.[1]

company until 1979, when she joined American Ballet Theatre. She appeared in numerous principal roles, including a summer's tour in 1981 as Alexander Godunov's partner, and has appeared on television a number of times. For the last eight years she has been gaining a broad reputation as a freelance choreographer, setting ballets for companies all over the world.

Sean Lavery is from Harrisburg, Pennsylvania, and also received early training at the Pennsylvania Ballet and at the Central Pennsylvania Youth Ballet. After a stint in New York at the Richard Thomas School he joined the San Francisco Ballet in 1973, and then the Frankfurt Opera Ballet in 1975. A year in New York at the School of American Ballet was followed by an invitation to join the New York City Ballet in 1977. He danced many principal roles with that company. After health problems forced him to retire from active dancing, he continued his activities in the ballet world as Ballet Master of the New York City Ballet, and has also choreographed some works.

The subjects for the more recent photographs for the new sections of this book are Julie Kent and Benjamin Pierce. Julie is a principal dancer with American Ballet Theatre, having joined the company first as an apprentice in 1985, and then as a company member in 1986. In 1985 she won first place in the regional finals of the National Society of Arts and Letters at the Kennedy Center, and in 1986 was the only American to win a medal at the Prix de Lausanne International Ballet Competition. Her roles with ABT include the leading role in *Ballet Imperial*, a Shade in *La Bayadère*, Prayer in *Coppélia*, Giselle and the peasant *pas de deux* in *Giselle*, Caroline in *Jardin aux lilas*, Juliet in *Romeo and Juliet*, the Lilac Fairy, Princess Florine, the Fairy of Generosity, and Diamond in *The Sleeping Beauty*, and many other roles. In 1987 she starred in the Herbert Ross film *Dancers*. Miss Kent's training included study with Hortensia Fonseca at the Academy of the Maryland Youth Ballet, and at the School of American Ballet.

Benjamin Pierce joined American Ballet Theatre in 1988, where he has danced roles in *La Bayadère*, *Concerto*, a toreador in Vladimir Vasiliev's staging of *Don Quixote*, Wilfred in *Giselle*, Fernando Bujones's staging of *Raymonda*, Act III, and others. His training began at age 5 in Bethesda, Maryland, and continued at the Pacific Northwest Ballet School, the National Ballet of Canada, the Washington School of Ballet, where he studied with Choo San Goh, and the School of American Ballet, where he

Julie Kent and Benjamin Pierce, the dancers who performed for the new photography for this book.

studied with Stanley Williams. He has danced principal roles in *The Sleeping Beauty*, *Napoli*, *Les Patineurs*, *The Four Temperaments*, and Balanchine's *The Nutcracker* in various school productions prior to his tenure at ABT.

Both Ms. Kent and Mr. Pierce appear in this book courtesy of American Ballet Theatre.

The photography for the book was done by Martha Swope, a name familiar to all who have contact with the dance world. Her photography has appeared in major publications from magazines to performance programs, in numerous books on dance, and in exhibits all over the world. Examples of her books are *The New York City Ballet*,[2] with text by Lincoln Kirstein, *Baryshnikov at Work*,[3] and *Martha Graham—Portrait of the Lady as an Artist*.[4] Martha Swope studied ballet for five years at the School of American Ballet, and modern dance for two years with Martha Graham. She served as official photographer for the New York City Ballet for over twenty years, and for American Ballet Theatre and Martha Graham for many years. She now photographs most of the Broadway shows each year.

Paul Harvath, whose photographs appear in chapter 12, is an official photographer for the U.S. Figure Skating Association. As skaters themselves, Paul and his wife, Michelle, provided valuable advice on the ice skating discussions in addition to contributing the photographs.

All of these artists were challenged to perform their jobs in a very unusual way. Lisa, Sean, Julie, and Ben, in addition to performing standard dance movements with the particular emphases needed to illustrate the analyses, were also asked to perform some movements incorrectly in order to illustrate such problems as off-balance *pirouettes* or "drooping" *arabesque* turns. Julie willingly performed "finger turns" on a steel platform with a mechanical bearing overhead instead of a partner's hand! They rose to these challenges with the skill, control, cooperation, and understanding that one can expect only from the most dedicated and confident artists. When movements had to be performed dozens of times in order to catch the right moments in a picture, their cooperation and consistency were remarkable. And Martha Swope was challenged to catch on film fleeting instants of movements that one does not usually see in dance photographs. The understanding and artistic sense of each of these artists have added immeasurably to this book.

The video cassette accompanying this book is primarily the

Catherine O'Brien and Martha Swope, video producer and photographer for this book project, respectively.

The authors discuss a technical point with Julie Kent during the photography.

work of Catherine O'Brien, head of Presto! Productions in New Hampshire, and Ron Wyman, of Atlantic Media Services. Ms. O'Brien is currently director of the Video/Media Group at Stanford University. Each invested many hard hours recording and editing the material seen in the cassette. They created the dynamic visual images needed to bring to life many of the concepts in this book.

Cynthia Harvey
Kenneth Laws

## Notes

1. Kenneth Laws, *The Physics of Dance* (New York: Schirmer Books, 1984).
2. Lincoln Kirstein, *The New York City Ballet*, illustrated by Martha Swope (New York: Alfred A. Knopf, 1973).
3. Mikhail Baryshnikov, *Baryshnikov at Work*, illustated by Martha Swope (New York: Alfred A. Knopf, 1978).
4. Leroy Leatherman, *Martha Graham—Portrait of the Lady as an Artist*, illustrated by Martha Swope (New York: Alfred A. Knopf, 1965).

*Physics, Dance, and the*
*Pas de Deux*

# 1

# *Introduction*

## The Role of Physical Analysis

Dance is an ephemeral art. Like music, it is temporal; unlike music, it depends on both visual and aural senses of the observer. The essence of music is the organization of sound; the heart of dance is the presentation of moving human bodies, usually in conjunction with music.

We respond to music because we share some common experience with the musician. Although many of us are not musical, and many do not play musical instruments, we are surrounded by music in our culture. But each of us does have a voice. Is it any wonder that popular music is almost always vocal? And since we each have a body, we can all respond to the visual images created by people moving with the intent of sharing those images with us. We respond vicariously to what we can imagine ourselves doing. And it is particularly appealing to respond to performers who carry out their craft with obvious skill, whether as singers or as dancers.

The dancer's primary aim is to project an aesthetic image to an audience. The means by which dancers project that image can

FIGURE 1-1   Author Cynthia Harvey performs with Guillaume Graffin in Kenneth MacMillan's *Manon* for American Ballet Theatre.

be described, understood, and appreciated on different levels, one of which involves the mechanics of how bodies move under the influence of forces exerted on them.

Most dance enthusiasts—dancers, teachers, choreographers, and spectators—consider dance to be a purely aesthetic performing art. They recognize that the challenge for the dancer is to communicate to an audience the visual images intended by the choreographer and the dancer. Many also realize that part of the enjoyment of dance depends on recognizing the difficulty of performing these movements well, making physically challenging movements appear smooth and graceful. Some analyze dance movement in terms of choreographic principles or aesthetic motivation; others take the further step of analyzing movements physically in order to understand the mechanics of dance from the perspective of the dancer. Why are certain movements particularly difficult? Which movements are illusions that appear to violate fundamental physical principles? How do dancers create these illusions? How do they use physical principles of motion to their advantage, rather than fighting against them? How do two dancers interact to produce movement and images impossible for either to accomplish alone?

There are many in the dance community who do analyze dance movement, but in a different way. One approach is that of Rudolf von Laban, who created a structure in which dance movement can be codified or categorized. Movements are analyzed in terms of, for instance, the quality of movement—"gliding," "punching," "pressing"; and the use of space—higher or lower, right or left. The aesthetic imagery determines the basis for categorization of body movements.

The physical analysis that is the focus of this book assumes that the motivation for a particular type of movement is already established, and the questions involve what the body has to do physically to create that movement, and what movements are constrained by the way masses move through space under the influence of the various forces acting on them.

As an example of the way physical understanding can contribute to a deeper appreciation of dance, consider a dancer performing a *tour jeté*—a turning leap. No matter how much that dancer may wish to leap off the floor and *then* start turning, the law of conservation of rotational momentum tells us that such a maneuver is absolutely impossible. So how does a dancer perform this impressive movement? There is a subtle way the dancer controls body configuration so that the movement creates the *illusion* of a turn that occurs only after the dancer has risen into the air. Understanding the way the physical principles apply to this movement not only gives the dancer the reasons for the most effective technique, but also provides the observer with a deeper understanding of the dancer's skill in carrying out the movement.

There is an understandable fear that the aesthetic impact of dance may be sacrificed if one tries to analyze the art form scientifically. A newspaper dance critic reporting on a scientific study of *pirouettes* headed his article "He wants to reduce ballet to a science."[1] (Actually, the investigator was *not* ignoring the aesthetic dimension and the essence of communication with an audience.) As philosopher Susanne Langer put it:

> In watching a dance, you do not see what is physically before you—people running around or twisting their bodies; what you see is a display of interacting forces. . . . But these forces . . . are not the physical forces of the dancer's muscles. . . . The forces we seem to perceive most directly and convincingly are created for our perception; and they exist only for it.[2]

Some dancers may feel that science doesn't really apply to aesthetic art forms. Bart Cook, a member of the New York City Ballet, was quoted several years ago in a *Dance Magazine* interview as saying "It's that vision of freedom you create when you're defying physical law . . . ."[3] And Lisa de Ribère, a former soloist with American Ballet Theatre, who has submitted her talents to scientific scrutiny, has said that an understanding of physical principles is useful to a dancer in developing technique, but that the *last* thing she would want to think about when on stage in front of an audience is controlling her moment of inertia or maximizing her rotational momentum in a turn! During performance, artistic sensitivities *must* occupy a dancer's full attention.

Since a focus exclusively on physical analysis may detract from performance or appreciation of dance as an art form, what *is* the value of such analysis? The value of one aspect of analysis has been gaining acceptance in the past several years. Dancers, dance teachers, and people in the medical professions are now recognizing the importance of a knowledge of anatomy for allowing dancers to use their bodies most effectively and safely. A knowledge of anatomical limitations and constraints on human

body movement can help prevent the kinds of injuries that interrupt or end many promising dance careers. And clearly teachers benefit from understanding how the muscles work in dance movement, what constraints are imposed by muscles and bones, and to what extent a young dance student can expand the range of motion permitted by these constraints. An example is a *grand battement devant* in which the structure of the hip prevents maintaining a complete turn-out through the upper range of the motion (figure 1-2). The good teacher knows and teaches the ideal positions and body configurations, but recognizes the distinction between the ideal and the possible. Teaching involves a balance between eliciting the best possible technique from dancers and recognizing human limits.

But analyzing dance can contribute more fundamentally to the skill a dancer uses in creating this art. Although dancers cannot see themselves totally in physical terms, as massive bodies moving through space under the influence of well-known forces and obeying physical laws, neither can they afford to ignore these aspects of movement. According to Allegra Fuller Snyder, former head of the Dance Department at UCLA:

> Dance is more than an art. It is one of the most powerful tools for fusing the split between the two functions of the brain—the fusing of the logical with the intuitive, the fusing of the analytical perceptions with the sensorial perceptions, the fusing of holistic understanding with step-by-step thinking. It is a discipline which within itself deals with basic understanding of human experience, and conceptualization.[4]

Dancers are unavoidably aware of the mechanics of movement. Gravity and other aspects of one's physical surroundings do affect how dancers move. And movements must *work* physically in order for aesthetic imagery to be expressed. An ethereal, floating image will never result from a woman being lifted if the lift is impossible for her and her partner to perform smoothly. A climactic sudden stop at the end of a fast and energetic *pirouette* will lose its impact if there is no mechanism for quickly getting rid of the momentum of the turning motion. The mechanics of the movement must work hand in hand with the aesthetic intent of the choreography.

Only when the movements called for by the choreography work within the constraints of physical reality and of the technical capabilities of the dancers can the dancers apply their interpretive skills in order to *dance*, and not just go through the

FIGURE 1-3    The balances required of the ballerina in the "Rose Adagio" from *The Sleeping Beauty* require considerable technical facility.

motions. Then, of course, dancers strive to free their minds from concerns about the mechanics of movement, and think about dance, movement, partner, and music, rather than force, balance, inertia, and momentum.

It must be noted that an understanding of the mechanical principles that apply to dance movement does not automatically allow dancers to perform movements otherwise beyond their ability. The understanding may be profound and the spirit willing, and the body may *still* not cooperate! The technique for achieving the balances in the "Rose Adagio" of *The Sleeping Beauty* may be grasped, but accomplishing those balances, as shown in figure 1-3, is still very difficult.

The emphasis in this book is almost entirely on movements of *classical ballet*, not because of a judgment as to the inherent value or worth of that style of dance, but because of the relatively well-defined and accepted "vocabulary" of movements and positions. Although there are variations in the style with which balletic movements are carried out by different dancers working from different choreographers, there is a fundamentally "correct" way of performing a *tour jeté*, a *pirouette en dehors*, or a *cabriole en avant*. Analyses of these movements therefore have a generalizable applicability that is potentially useful for any dancer performing any dance movements.

Modern, jazz, or ballroom dance, and even some forms of folk dance share with ballet many similarities in the types of movements on which these styles are based. Turns on one foot are turns whether executed in balletic form with the gesture leg in a *retiré* position or with some other body position called for by the style of the dance. Jumps, leaps, partnered lifts, balance positions, and essentially any other type of dance movement imaginable can be analyzed using the techniques described in the following chapters. Ballet is merely the most convenient vehicle for the analyses since it is the most well defined, constant, and universal style of dance, and the form of dance most familiar to the authors.

## Physics and Dance

The science of physics deals with the motion and interaction of material bodies. Its development over the centuries has given rise to laws of motion that are always observed to be valid with a high degree of accuracy. With careful analyses these laws can be applied to dance movement with results that are intriguing, instructive, useful, and at times surprising. The aim in this book is not only to create a collection of analyzed movements, but to articulate the techniques of analysis so that the reader can extend these techniques to other instances in the infinite variety of body movements observed in dance and other human activity.

How is the role of physics in dance best demonstrated? Mathematical equations are useful only when insight into the applicable physical principles is already established. Thus, most of the material in this book deals with conceptual descriptions and illustrations of the application of physical laws. Some of the more detailed or quantitative discussions appear in the appendixes.

The field of biomechanics involves an analysis of the movement of bodies (usually human) in terms of the concepts of mechanics. But those principles are applied as much to the anatomy of the body and its internal workings as to the way the body moves in response to external forces. Since physics usually deals with objects moving in response to external influences, the subject matter of this book is identified as the *physics* of dance. Most of the applications of physics dealt with in this book have to do with the response of the body to the external forces that lead to movement.

Dance consists of both movement and line or position; it has both dynamic and static aspects. To which aspect is the aesthetic quality attributable? The eye clearly sees both instantaneous line or position *and* movement, but are they both perceived simultaneously, or does the mind emphasize one or the other at a particular time? Can the mind see a series of body positions and moving images simultaneously, or does it attend to one or the other aesthetic aspect at a time?

There is a principle of physics called the "Principle of Complementarity" that applies to observations of small particles or waves. Particles are associated with well-defined positions; waves are associated with movement, but may not be localizable to specific positions. Particles exhibit aspects of waves, and waves exhibit aspects of particles. But according to the Principle of Complementarity, one can see the wavelike properties (movement) of an entity clearly only if one sacrifices seeing at the same time the particle-like aspects (position) and vice versa. Thus one can accurately measure an entity's position only if its state of motion is not simultaneously measured with great accuracy. Perhaps the eye and mind have a similar "complementarity" when dance is observed, effectively "seeing" only positions *or* movement, but not both simultaneously.

One of the challenges in dealing with technical aspects of dance, whether ballet or some other form, involves the uses of appropriate vocabulary and terminology. How is a basis for communication established between such disparate fields as physics and dance? One characteristic of science is that it is built on precise definitions of pertinent terms. These definitions are intended to be as objective as possible so that they are universally usable, independent of the unique interpretations of individuals. Physicists may disagree on interpretations of observations, but they depend on an assumed agreement concerning the definitions of the terms.

People dealing with dance depend on language to serve two functions. The first is to be a vehicle for communicating ideas from one person to another, and the second is to form meaningful images in terms of dancers' individual senses of body and movement. A dance teacher may use words that have objective definitions, but unless students can translate those words into images applicable to their own bodies, the transfer of information is abstract and not useful.

Individual students, because of different ages and backgrounds, have different levels and kinds of understanding. Dance teachers, who often deal with young people who have not developed a sophisticated vocabulary, create images that seem to work, building on common understandings of how it "feels" to perform certain movements or maintain certain body positions. "Feel as if your body is squeezed into a drinking straw" may be translated by some students into "Maintain a compact alignment around a vertical axis in order to perform a controlled turn." Or, more physical yet, "Minimize your rotational inertia around a vertical axis so that the torque and rotational momentum needed for a given rate of turn will be minimized." The message is the same; the frame of reference is determined by the student's background and intellectual capacity. (The physical principles applicable to this movement—the *pirouette*—are discussed in chapter 4 and appendixes A and B.)

When learning or improving a particular movement, a dancer usually depends on three methods: trial and error, as adjustments are made in the basic motions; the example of an experienced dancer executing the motion correctly; and instructions from a teacher or peer. The instructions are often based on an idea of what makes the movement "right." Although the validity of these traditional methods of learning has been well proved historically, an additional basis for learning is a more analytical understanding of how a particular body position or movement contributes to the desired form or action.

The example described above, involving placement for a *pirouette*, may be extended. An instructor may tell a student to stretch vertically, pushing into the floor with the supporting foot while reaching for the ceiling with the head. Now, if the vertical height of the center of gravity is constant, then the vertical force of the dancer's foot against the floor is no greater or less than the body weight. But the image produced by that instruction elicits a response in the dancer that results in a strong and straight vertical alignment, which makes the *pirouettes* more successful. And the student observes dancers with weak or flaccid backs having trouble with *pirouettes*. An analysis shows why these aspects of body placement contribute to successful *pirouettes*. If the body is properly "pulled up," its mass is held close to the axis of rotation, decreasing the rotational inertia (see appendix B) and allowing for a substantial rate of turn. Mass displaced from the rotation axis also contributes to a wobbling, since that mass tends to be thrown out from the axis by a centrifugal effect. Such placement is thus not only desirable for aesthetic reasons, but also necessary in order to achieve a reasonable turn rate and smooth, stable rotation.

Although difficult physical feats are often accomplished by pure strength and agility, it is sometimes true that the appearance of performing certain movements is illusory, and a deeper skill is required of the dancer in creating these illusions. For the dancer or dance teacher, a physical analysis of movement provides a basis for developing techniques for creating or enhancing the illusion of performing the impossible.

It is also true that an *observer* watching a dance performance can appreciate dance movement more deeply with an understanding of the limitations imposed by physical law and of the role of illusion. Dance movement often inspires awe in the observer, not only because of the beauty of the moving human form, but also because the dancer seems to defy the normal physical constraints nature imposes on moving objects. An understanding of the appropriate physical principles allows the spectator to distinguish between possible and impossible movements, and to appreciate the subtle skill of a dancer who creates the illusion of performing the impossible.

What physical principles are pertinent to an analysis of dance? We must first agree that the physical laws that have been shown to apply to objects moving in response to gravity and other forces *do* indeed apply to the moving human body, even though that body can change its own shape and the forces it exerts on its surroundings. We must therefore deal with the concepts of force, energy, momentum, inertia, velocity, and acceleration in the same careful way that these concepts have been applied to inanimate objects. The challenge is to analyze physically what *can* be analyzed in terms of appropriate physical principles, while not losing sight of the significance of the dancer's own experience—what the dancer *feels* as interactions with the world take place. The dancer ultimately controls movement by controlling his or her interaction with the outside world. A dancer's mind determines how and when muscles are going to be activated in order to produce motion. We are considering here what happens physically when the dancer has decided to move in a particular way.

Newton's laws of motion form the basis of any analysis of massive objects in motion. Conservation of linear and rotational momentum and the relationship between forces and the resulting changes in the state of motion are principles derived from Newton's laws. ("Force" is a term that quantifies the concept of a push or pull. "Momentum" represents a *quantity* of motion, best defined mathematically. "Linear" involves movement along a line, while "rotational" refers to turning motion around an axis. See appendixes A and B. Note that in dance, "rotation" sometimes refers to the turn-out, or an orientation of the legs that is rotated outward around their longitudinal axes. In this book "rotation" means the turning *motion* of any object such as the body.) These principles and laws are deceptively simple to state but enormously powerful when they are carefully applied. Such simplicity and power are sources of awesome beauty in a science such as physics.

When one is dancing alone, earth's gravity and the floor are the only sources of force acting on one's body. All changes in the state of movement of the dancer as a whole are dependent on the unavoidable effect of gravity, which cannot be controlled by the dancer, and must involve interactions between the body and the floor, which usually *can* be controlled. That is, the earth is pulling down on the body with a constant force; nothing one does can change that. But one can interact with the floor in such a way as to maintain balance, or jump, or start moving in some direction, or start turning. Accomplishing those aims involves not only the thought process that tells the muscles to exert themselves in particular ways, and with a particular intensity or speed, but also must involve an interaction with the "outside world." In the case of the solo dancer, the "outside world" is gravity and the floor.

Dance movement can be broken down into categories that

FIGURE 1-4   A partner can provide a source of force other than the floor and gravity, allowing a dancer to achieve positions not possible when dancing alone.

involve characteristic techniques of analysis. Some movements involve primarily vertical or horizontal motions of the body as a whole, in which rotations can be ignored. These motions can be studied using simple equations of linear motion in three dimensions. The resulting analysis leads to a recognition and understanding of some interesting illusions and techniques, such as the appearance of floating horizontally in a *grand jeté*. Rotational motions require different approaches, involving the way the body's mass is distributed, different axes of rotation for different types of movement, and sources of forces that produce the rotational motion. The simplest rotational motions are *pirouettes* of all types, but there are other movements that involve rotations around horizontal axes (*entrechats*) or skewed axes (*tour jetés*). These will be discussed in chapters 3 and 5.

Physical analyses can make important contributions to an understanding of the effects of the size of dancers on the movements they can perform. Most choreographers and teachers recognize that small dancers do have different ways of moving than taller ones, but just what are the differences? How can teachers avoid expecting the impossible of tall dancers, or choreographers maximize the effectiveness of their use of performers of different sizes? Are there physical principles that make the slender, long-legged "Balanchine" dancers particularly appropriate for Balanchine choreography? Is there a way to choreograph specifically for the talented but "undersize" dancers who can outperform their taller counterparts in particular movements and tempos? Physical analyses can answer many of these questions.

When partners are working together in a *pas de deux*, there is physical contact between the two bodies. The sources of interaction between the dancer and the "outside world" now include a partner in addition to gravity and the floor. Those interaction forces between partners are controlled by two different minds, each with its own motivation, interpretation, timing, and strength. A partnered dancer now experiences forces that are no longer totally under his or her control, or even predictable, unlike interactions with the floor or with gravity. And the timing and magnitude of those forces from the partner may depend not only on the partner's capabilities but also on that individual's mental state and personal interpretation of the music, which may change from one performance to the next. These vagaries can create an uncertainty in partnering that adds to the difficulty for the dancers, but can also add the excitement of spontaneity that may inspire strong responses from an audience.

How are the concepts of movement analysis dealt with in a medium as static as a book? Good dance photography involves a subtle challenge to portray movement with static visual displays. The challenge is particularly crucial when the purpose of the photography is to illustrate the applicability of physical principles that apply mostly to movement. The transitions and accelerations from one configuration to the next are particularly amenable to physical analysis, and are particularly fruitful in contributing to an understanding of dance movement. But how does one illustrate these transitions visually? Is it possible for a static image to portray a transitory moment without destroying the aesthetic sense of the position as inseparable from the movement accompanying it? An example is a *tombé* movement, which is discussed in chapter 3 (and illustrated in figures 2–6 and 3–4) as it contributes to a horizontal acceleration away from a balance condition. A still photograph of the movement in progress shows the lean of the body that is related to the acceleration, but does it look like dance? The viewer has to imagine the motion associated with the position in order to grasp the full significance of the illustration. The photographs and diagrams in this book represent the most accessible, though imperfect, way of presenting those visual images. The accompanying video cassette provides a dynamic, and therefore more complete, representation of the movements analyzed.

Although the principles that apply to dance movement are the focus of this book, the intent is not to provide a "how to" guide that a novice can use to learn dance technique. The movements described and illustrated are those seen in the movement vocabulary of professional dancers, and require substantial skilled training. Some of these movements, particularly those involving partners, can be dangerous, and should not be attempted without the appropriate training.

Certainly dance cannot be "reduced to a science." But the world of dance is large and complex, with many windows through which one can both perceive and illuminate. Through these windows one may see portrayals of characters or images of a culture, spectacular athleticism or lyrical grace, painful years of dancers' discipline, or free expression of human creativity. We hope that the view through the window of physical analysis will enhance, not detract from, the depth of appreciation this art form can stimulate, as well as contribute to the advancement of the art and skill of dance.

## Notes

1. Daniel Webster, "He wants to reduce ballet to a science," *Philadelphia Inquirer*, 4 April 1978, 4-B.
2. Susanne Langer, "The Dynamic Image: Some Philosophical Reflections on Dance," in *Problems of Art* (New York: Scribners, 1957), 5.
3. Tobi Tobias, "Bart Cook," *Dance Magazine* (September 1978), 59.
4. Allegra Fuller Snyder, unpublished address to the faculty of the Department of Dance, University of California at Los Angeles, Fall 1974.

# 2

# *Balance*

Any choreographed dance sequence consists of three components—movement, poses, and transitions. Movement is the heart of dance, and is primarily the aspect that characterizes the style and image that a dance conveys. Poses provide the breathing time and temporary still images that allow the performer or observer to absorb and digest what is happening. Transitions and the organization of these movements and poses are part of the challenge to the choreographer as a dance is created. Some of the more breathtaking moments in a dance occur when a dancer enters a pose, sometimes directly from a moving step, and holds the position while balanced *en pointe* for several heart-stopping seconds. A *pirouette* ending in a motionless, balanced pose is particularly impressive. Questions involving balance provide some particularly interesting, often misunderstood, sometimes surprising, but certainly useful applications of physical analysis.

One of the primary mechanical considerations in any sort of stationary position or pose is balance. What is meant by balance? How does a dancer alone achieve and maintain balance? When

FIGURE 2-1   Suzanne Farrell and Jacques d'Amboise in George Balanchine's *Diamonds* for the New York City Ballet.

partners are working together, who controls balance in different types of positions? (The last question will be discussed in chapter 8.)

## Static Balance

For our purposes, "balance" means that condition in which the body is in stationary equilibrium with no tendency to topple due to the effect of gravity. Mechanically, that means that the center of gravity—that point where the effective force of gravity may be considered to act on the body as a whole—must lie on a vertical line that passes through the area of support at the floor. Suppose a person is standing on two feet on the floor. In order to be balanced, the person's center of gravity must lie directly above the area circumscribed by the perimeter of the contact between the feet and the floor. Clearly, if that area is small, as when the feet are close together, or *very* small, as for a dancer on one foot *en pointe*, it is a great challenge to locate the center of gravity within the range of locations directly above that small area, and toppling off balance is hard to avoid. At the opposite extreme, the three-point stance of an offensive lineman in football (on two feet and one hand) is a very stable configuration.

What determines the location of the center of gravity? For a person in a normal standing position on two feet, the center of gravity is in the sagittal plane (the vertical plane that divides the left and right sides of the body), somewhere in the abdominal area. It is somewhat higher in the body in men than in women, due to greater hip mass in women and greater chest/shoulder mass in men. Now suppose part of the body, such as a leg, is extended to the side. That displacement of part of the mass of the body to the side will cause the center of gravity to be displaced to that side also. For the body as a whole to remain balanced, at least part of the mass of the rest of the body must be displaced in the opposite direction, which may give rise to an apparent lean of the balanced body away from the extended leg. In any balanced position, different dancers find that slightly different positions of the body work best, due to differences in body structure, flexibility, and comfort.

One major characteristic of the center of gravity is that it cannot be moved from rest unless some net force acts on the body as a whole. That is, one can move individual parts of the body relative to each other in many ways, but unless those movements result in a force between the body and the "outside world" (everything outside the body itself), then those movements cannot cause a change in the location of the center of gravity in space. If one is standing still on a floor, there *are* forces acting on the body—the downward force of gravity acting at the center of gravity, and the upward force of the floor supporting the person. But these two forces acting on the body balance each other, acting along the same vertical line, producing no net movement of the center of gravity. And if one is standing on ice with infinitely slippery shoes, there is no horizontal force, either, so no movement of the center of gravity of the body can occur.

Actually, one must say that unless the outside world exerts a force on a body, there is no *change in state of motion of the body*. That is, if the body's center of gravity is at rest, it will remain at rest. But if it is initially moving, it will remain in uniform motion until it is acted on by some outside force. For example, an ice skater moving in a straight line on almost frictionless ice will continue moving with constant speed as long as no forces act on the body. This powerful result is among the implications of the laws of Isaac Newton mentioned in chapter 1.

Suppose a dancer starts on one foot *en pointe*, in an *arabesque* position, as shown in the first view in figures 2-2. And suppose the dancer is initially balanced, as in figure 2-3, so that her center of gravity is on a vertical line that passes through the area of contact between her *pointe* shoe and the floor. If she is absolutely motionless, she could presumably remain there forever. But there *is* motion—breathing, heartbeat, and blood circulation, if nothing else. So it is likely that she will soon find herself slightly off balance, beginning to topple, as in the second view in figure 2-2.

If the center of gravity is close to that "balance area," the acceleration away from the vertical is initially quite small. In other words, the closer a dancer is to a perfect balance, the slower will be the fall away from balance. If there is a small initial angle by which the line from the support to the center of mass is displaced from the vertical, that angle will increase at an accelerating rate. The calculations described in appendix E are applied to the geometry of a typical dancer. The results show that the angle of departure from the vertical increases by a factor of about eight in one second after the initial "almost balanced"

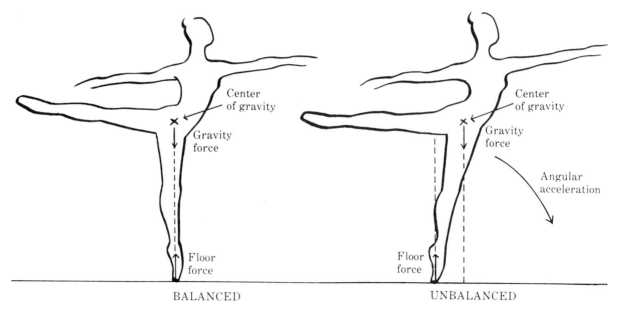

FIGURE 2-2 Forces acting on the body that result in balance or in a toppling away from balance.

moment. If the initial angle is 1°, the angle after one second will be about 8°, whereas if the initial angle is 4°, the body one second later makes an angle of more than 30° from the vertical, clearly a situation requiring some corrective action! Since these two examples represent a difference in initial position of the center of gravity of perhaps 2 inches, the initial placement of the body must be quite accurate if temporary balance is to be achieved.

## Regaining Balance

Let's assume this dancer wishes to remain balanced. What, if anything, can she do to regain balance? There are only two mechanisms for such adjustment. The point of support (or, more accurately, the *area* of support) at the floor must be shifted so that it falls directly under the center of gravity. Or, alternatively, the center of gravity must be shifted so that it is over the area of support at the floor.

The location of the contact area between the foot and the floor can be controlled. Of course, the dancer may hop, shifting the horizontal position of the entire supporting foot. But a more

FIGURE 2-3 Julie Kent in a balanced *arabesque* position.

subtle adjustment is possible. The center of force may be defined as that point where a distributed force or a collection of several forces may be considered to act, in terms of its effect on a body. When one balances on a flat foot, one can feel the foot moving in such a way as to make small corrections in the location of that center of force within the area of support, thereby maintaining the center of support under the center of gravity, as shown in figure 2-4. A dancer *en pointe*, however, has such a small area of contact with the floor that it is quite difficult to shift the center of force. The difficulty of the required manipulation is one reason dancing *en pointe* requires strong feet and ankles and much skill.

The other technique for regaining balance involves shifting the location of the center of gravity back toward the vertical line above the contact area at the floor. We have noted that controlling the location of the center of gravity requires some force from the "outside world" acting on the body, so no manipula-

FIGURE 2-4  Shifting the center
of supporting force at the floor
in order to control balance.

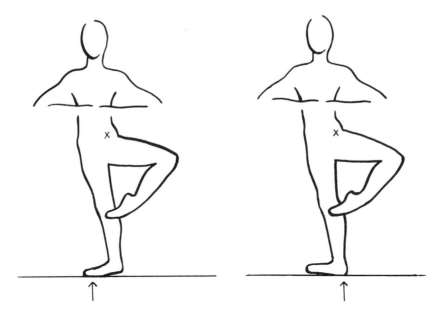

tion of the body will accomplish the desired end unless it results
in such a force. A remarkable implication of that fact is that it
does no good merely to try to move a massive part of the body
in the desired direction directly. That may only result in some
other part of the body being displaced in the opposite direction.

There is an interesting experiment one can do alone. Imagine
that you are standing at the edge of the roof of a building, on
your toes, facing the precipice. You start toppling forward, as if
someone has given you a gentle push from behind. How does
your body react to keep you from falling over the edge? Those
with insufficient imaginative powers may just take a step forward, correcting the imbalance because there is actually no precipice there, but solid floor. Others with a keen but incomplete
sense of mechanical analysis may move the upper body backwards, recognizing that a movement of body mass backwards
must be accomplished in order to move the center of gravity
back toward the balance location. Over they go!

The ones who succeed in correcting the imbalance are those
who relax and find that an automatic reaction of the body takes
over. They actually bend the upper body suddenly *forward* from
the waist, as shown in figure 2-5, and perhaps also rotate the
arms in a windmill fashion (forward and down, back and up).
Why do those movements succeed? The body is trying to conserve its rotational momentum around a horizontal axis through

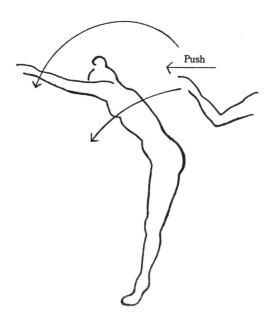

Push

the center of gravity in the abdominal area. (See appendix B for a discussion of the conservation of rotational momentum.) If the upper body is rotating forward from the hips, and perhaps the arms are rotating in the same direction (counterclockwise as viewed from the person's left), the rest of the body will try to rotate in the opposite direction (clockwise as viewed from the left). Thus, the legs will try to rotate forward from the hips, pushing forward with the feet against the surface on which the person is standing. But that results in the surface exerting a force backward against the person's feet. If that's the only horizontal force acting on the body, it will act in such a way as to move the center of gravity backward, returning it toward the balance condition! Thus the reaction of the body—moving the upper body in the direction of the fall—is surprisingly the movement that works, and the mechanism can be understood on the basis of known physical principles. The windmilling arms accomplish the same purpose; that is, they represent a part of the body rotating counterclockwise that causes the rest of the body—specifically, the legs—to try to rotate in the opposite direction, again resulting in the backward push of the floor against the feet.

Although dancers may intuitively realize that it *is* possible to regain balance while supported on one foot, they may fail to recognize that it is not the manipulations of the body directly that restore balance, but the horizontal force exerted on the

*Balance*

*21*

floor that accomplishes the shift in position of the center of gravity. That is, movements of the body that maximize the horizontal force of the supporting foot against the floor will be most effective in restoring (or destroying) balance. Unless such movements can be learned, or applied from natural instincts, the body may move in counterproductive ways, preventing the desired adjustment in balance. In fact, the natural and correct reaction for regaining balance, as described above, has been claimed to be wrong, and dancers have been admonished to overcome that "instinct" and merely move the body back toward balance![1] Such action would clearly be counterproductive. Fortunately, most people, including dancers, have developed a valid automatic reaction, probably learned in early childhood, for regaining or maintaining balance.

Dancers can be observed to carry out those necessary adjustments when trying to balance alone. Of course, the movements are subtle because dancers, among all categories of people who depend on control of body movement for their activity, are perhaps *most* sensitive to the condition of balance or loss thereof.

There are other examples of regaining balance. Have you ever walked along a rail of a railroad track, trying to maintain balance? You have probably found that if you start falling to your right, your upper body will suddenly bend toward the right. By the same explanation as described above, that movement results in the rail exerting a horizontal force on your body toward the left, helping to return you to the balance condition.

## Acceleration away from Balance

The same principles apply when a dancer desires to accelerate away from a balance condition. Perhaps you have seen a dancer get "stuck" in balance and have to drop out of the pose in order to start moving to the next step. Again the necessary action is either (1) to shift the location of the center of force at the floor in order to initiate toppling or (2) to move the body in such a way as to exert a force on the floor in a direction opposite to the direction of motion so that the floor can provide the necessary accelerating force *in* the direction of desired motion. If one is off balance leaning to the right, it is clearly easy to push against the floor to the left in order to accelerate to the right. But suppose one is initially balanced? An example of an appropriate movement, which of course must be part of the choreography, occurs when a dancer is initially balanced in *arabesque*, and then swings the gesture leg down and forward, in a *tombé* movement. In this movement, often used when initiating a horizontal motion, the gesture leg rotates forward around a horizontal axis through the hip. (Anatomically this would be called motion in the sagittal plane about a transverse axis.) The rest of the body, trying to conserve rotational momentum, automatically reacts by trying to rotate in the opposite direction. This reaction of the rest of the body causes the supporting foot to try to move backward against the floor, resulting in a forward force from the floor on the body, producing the forward acceleration of the body. (The process of accelerating away from a static position will be discussed in more detail in chapter 3.)

## Balance While Rotating

An interesting situation arises when the dancer performs a *pirouette* while maintaining balance. Is it possible for an unbalanced, *rotating* dancer to make the subtle corrections necessary to return to a balanced condition?

The first question is whether the toppling motion and body manipulations that maintain balance can be separated from the rotational motion or whether there would result some complicated motion of the kind observed when a spinning top wobbles if off balance (called "precession" in physics). The analysis described in appendix F shows that the rotational motion *can* be ignored when considering balance in normal *pirouettes*.

The challenge for the rotating, unbalanced dancer is to try to shift the body position in a subtle way so as to accomplish the same adjustment when rotating that was described earlier for the nonrotating situation. The task is made much more difficult by the rotation, because the adjustment, which must have a particular orientation and direction in space, must change relative to the body's orientation as the body turns. For instance, suppose the body is off balance, leaning toward stage right while turning to the right. The body must adjust its position in such a way that the floor will exert a horizontal force on the body toward stage left in order to shift the center of gravity back to the vertical line over the area of support. But stage left—the direction the body must move to regain balance—is to the dancer's left when she is facing front, to her rear when she is facing stage right, to her right when she is facing upstage, and so on. The necessary body adjustments are illustrated by Lisa de Ribère in the poses shown in figure 2-6. Is it possible for a dancer to make these adjustments that must change direction relative to the body as the turn occurs? That is a lot to expect when a turn involves a rotation of perhaps two or three revolutions per second! But if such an adjustment is *not* possible, then the dancer must begin the turn sufficiently close to balance that such adjustments are unnecessary. That also is a lot to expect of a dancer! A relaxed upper body is necessary to allow for the subtle body adjustments, but a strong lower body provides the support that prevents unwanted "wavering."

So how is it possible for some dancers to accomplish a multiple *pirouette* of a dozen or so turns without falling? The answer probably involves a combination of factors. First, the dancer does have to be close enough to balance that at least the first few turns can be accomplished with no adjustment. These turns may indeed be rapid enough that there is some stabilizing effect, as with a spinning top that remains upright because it is spinning. (Such a rapid turn with a rigid body is performed by an ice skater doing very rapid spins.) But as the turns become slower because of friction, one can look for those shifts of body position that do change direction as the body turns. This can be observed in a dancer skilled at *pirouettes* who is asked to try to maintain a turn even when falling out of it. The strange body adjustments in turns that are significantly off balance can be observed to rotate as the body rotates. It is true that such adjusting motions must occur so rapidly that they may be impossible to teach, meaning that certain people who are "natural" turners have, or can feel and develop, the proper reactions, and others must depend on initial accurate balance in order to accomplish the more usual two- or three-turn *pirouettes*.

FIGURE 2-6   The body's reaction to an off balance *pirouette* must rotate relative to the body as the body rotates. These four posed views, although exaggerated, show the directions of body adjustments that must be made to correct balance in a *pirouette* off balance to the left of the picture. Viewed in a clockwise order, these photos represent an *en dehors pirouette* turning to the right.

## A Final Look

The fundamental techniques used here for analyzing situations involving balance can be applied to an infinite variety of positions. The sources of forces and torques that maintain balance must be identified, then the action of the body that will cause the required forces to be exerted must be found. For the situations described in this chapter, there are a number of ways dancers and dance teachers can think about solutions to the problems. First, if one is to achieve a condition of balance, the center of gravity of one's body must be on a vertical line that passes within the area of support. In an *arabesque penchée*, for instance, in which the mass of the body shifts forward as the leg rises toward the vertical and the torso leans forward, there must be a conscious effort to allow the hip area to shift to the rear so that the body's center of gravity remains over the supporting foot. The situation is somewhat different with the support of a partner, as will be discussed in chapter 8.

When the condition of balance is not quite met, the body can carry out adjusting motions so as to regain balance. These adjustments require either a shift in the center of vertical supporting force at the floor or a push horizontally against the floor in a direction such as to cause the body's center of gravity to return to the balance configuration. The former is accomplished by adjustments in the supporting ankle or foot, the latter by shifting the upper body *toward* the direction of fall. Relaxation of the upper body can contribute to a sensitivity to slight displacements from balance, and make the small subtle adjustments smoother.

Horizontal acceleration away from balance is achieved either by shifting the center of supporting force (by lifting the lead foot, for example), or by a *tombé* or other movement that results in a horizontal force against the floor. Again, the horizontal force against the floor is the important factor. Balancing while rotating is made difficult by the fact that the direction of adjustment necessary to regain lost balance must shift relative to the body if it is to have the desired direction fixed relative to the world. That is, if the body is tending to fall toward stage right, the direction of adjustments in body position must remain such as to restore the body toward stage left even while the body is rotating relative to the stage.

What does an observer of dance see when a dancer achieves

impressive balances that seem to last forever? Is the dancer thinking, "Gee, I seem to be falling to my right, so I know I must quickly move my upper body to the right in order to exert a force toward the right between my feet and the floor so that the floor exerts a force to the left on my body, returning me to the balance condition in which my center of mass is on a vertical line passing through my support at the floor"? Probably not! But somewhere in the mind of the dancer there is an automatic response that accomplishes exactly that. Isn't it remarkable that the body is capable of that sort of response, particularly in the case of dancers, who are known to be particularly sensitive to balance and particularly adept at maintaining balance?

The series of *arabesque penchées* on a sloping ramp in *La Bayadère,* a long-held *arabesque* pose *en pointe* in the Sugar Plum Fairy *pas de deux* from *The Nutcracker*, or Giselle's shifting *attitude* position while hopping *en pointe* along a diagonal—all have similar requirements in terms of balance that can be understood using these principles. The same principles apply to the infinite variety of balanced poses seen in other styles of dance.

## Note

1. Norman Thomson, "The Barre—Aid or Crutch?," *Dance Magazine* (March 1981): 88-89.

# 3

# *Motions Without Turns*

We now move from balance and poses, which deal with the conditions of equilibrium of the dancer's body in an environment that includes the force of gravity, to the simplest movements—those involving linear movements, but no rotational motions such as *pirouettes*. The first step is, of course, starting the body moving from rest, which requires that a force act on it. A special case of acceleration involves moving in a curved path, such as running in a circular path around the stage, perhaps with turning *coupés jetés*. An acceleration, meaning a change in velocity, is also occurring when a moving body slows or stops. Another nonrotating category of movement is vertical jumps. What is the nature of the connection between height of a jump and time in the air?

Some of the more impressive movements in the dance repertoire involve traveling jumps such as *grands jetés*. How do dancers achieve an illusion in which they appear to float horizontally

FIGURE 3-1  Mikhail Baryshnikov in Twyla Tharp's *Push Comes to Shove* for American Ballet Theatre.

for a few moments near the peak of the jump? Jumps can be dangerous, particularly on floors that are not appropriate for dance. How do dancers accomplish landings that are gentle enough to avoid injury and do not result in slipping and falling? When and why is rosin useful in preventing slipping?

## Acceleration from Rest

First let us consider how a dancer can begin a movement from rest, involving a quick acceleration away from a standing position. As we found in the chapter on balance, if the body's center of gravity lies on a vertical line above the area of support, and there are no horizontal forces acting on the body, it will be in equilibrium and will remain at rest. If there *is* a net force, an acceleration of the body will occur that is proportional to the force and in the same direction.

Now, how does a person arrange to have a force exerted on himself in order to accelerate? For every force exerted by a body against something, the body experiences an equal and opposite force acting back on itself. (This is the third of a powerful set of laws of motion developed by Sir Isaac Newton in the seventeenth century, described in more detail in appendix A.) Since the floor is the only source of a force accessible to the dancer, he must arrange to push against it in order to accelerate. If he is initially balanced, it is not easy to exert that horizontal force. In fact, it may take too much time to develop sufficient acceleration to move into rapid running steps or other movements *and* remain with the music.

What does our dancer do to exert that force against the floor? One mechanism is to *shift the center of force between the feet and the floor*. Recall that the center of force is defined as the point where a distributed force, or a collection of several forces, may be considered to act. That is, if one's weight is distributed evenly over the supporting foot, which is flat on the floor, the center of force would be in the center of the foot. Leaning forward so that the weight is forward on the balls of the feet shifts the center of force toward the front of the foot. If the weight is distributed evenly between *two* feet, the center of force would be halfway between the feet; if more of the weight is borne by the front foot, the center of force would shift toward the front foot.

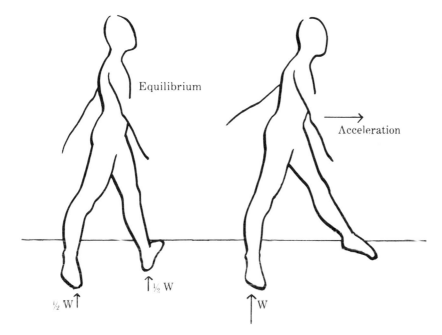

Equilibrium

Acceleration

½ W

↑½ W

↑W

Now suppose one wishes to accelerate forward from a standing position. If the feet are spread apart to the front and back, as in a lunge or a wide fourth position, merely lifting the front foot will shift the effective center of force to the rear. (See the diagrams in figure 3-2.) The center of gravity is then well in front of the support, and a fall to the front begins. The back foot can then exert a backwards push against the floor, resulting in an acceleration forward. That backwards force also counteracts the toppling forward.

If the feet are together at the beginning of the movement, the acceleration takes longer, since the center of force cannot be shifted as far horizontally. If the center of gravity is initially over the balls of the feet when the dancer is balanced, and then the fronts of the feet are lifted leaving the center of force back toward the heels, then the center of gravity will be slightly in front of the new center of force. A toppling rotation will start (as shown in figure 3-3) which can be counteracted by a backward horizontal force exerted by the feet against the floor. That force begins the linear acceleration forward. But because the center of gravity is only slightly in front of the center of force, the toppling rate will be small, and the horizontal force that can be exerted by the feet against the floor is small. If that force is too large, the

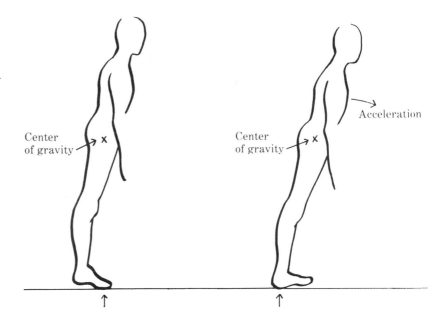

Center of gravity

Center of gravity

Acceleration

feet will simply run out from under the body, destroying equilibrium. The horizontal force must be just great enough to counteract the toppling.

A familiar example of this mechanism for acceleration is the starting position for a sprinter. Much of the runner's weight is forward on the hands, so that when the hands are lifted, the center of gravity is far forward of the supporting feet, and a large horizontal accelerating force can be exerted by the feet without the feet running out from under the rest of the body. Note, however, that a racing dive in swimming does not allow for as rapid an acceleration, because the distance through which the center of force can be shifted is limited by the small size of the diving platform.

The second mechanism for accelerating from rest involves *thrusting one leg front*, as in a *dégagé* movement, often seen at the beginning of a moving combination, and illustrated by Sean Lavery in figure 3-4. This movement causes the other (back) foot to push backward against the floor, resulting in the floor exerting a frontward accelerating force on the body. This mechanism can exist only for the short time that one part of the body (the gesture leg in this case) is *accelerating* relative to the rest of the body. It is therefore less effective, and is usually used along with the "shifting center of force" mechanism for causing horizontal accelerations.

FIGURE 3-4 Sean Lavery performing a *tombé*, or lunge, that allows for a horizontal acceleration

A motionless dancer, then, in order to accelerate rapidly with the first beat of the music, must quickly exert a backward force against the floor. The weight should be forward on the toes, or, better yet, one foot should be well in front of the other. Lifting the front foot will allow for a fast acceleration from the initial position. The movement will be more effective if the dancer also swings the front leg frontward as the acceleration begins. And of course all of these general principles can be applied to accelerations to the side or back.

*Motions Without Turns*

## Motion in a Curved Path

Technically, the term "acceleration" refers to any change in velocity, whether an increase or a decrease in speed *or* a change in the *direction* of motion. Any of these accelerations requires a force acting on the dancer from outside the body. One such horizontal acceleration involves motion in a circular path. That motion may be the running around the stage described earlier, possibly with other superimposed movements. Racing tracks are banked at the curves to allow the appropriate horizontal accelerating force to be exerted without resulting in a skid.

As we have seen, in order for a dancer to achieve a horizontal acceleration, the center of gravity must be displaced from the vertical line over the center of support at the floor, so that the floor can exert a horizontal force. As a dancer travels around the stage in a circular path, there must be a force on the body from the floor directed toward the center of the circle. That force will cause the constant change in direction of motion that is needed for the curved path. Because of the significant velocity, and because the circle diameter is restricted by the stage size, a sizable lean toward the center is often needed to prevent moving off the circle "on a tangent," perhaps leaving the stage precipitously. Note Sean's lean in figure 3-5, in which he is performing the curved-path motion described. The angle of lean can be calculated, and is in fact independent of the dancer's height, weight, or shape. If he is traveling at about 15 feet per second (half the speed of a sprinter) in a circle of diameter 30 feet, he must lean toward the center at an angle of 25° from the vertical! The horizontal force between his feet and the floor must be almost half of his weight. The frictional properties of floors that allow that magnitude of horizontal force will be discussed shortly.

Note that no change in horizontal speed *or direction* is possible during the flight phase of a traveling jump, when there is no contact with the floor. Horizontal travel in a curved path before a jump will not result in a curved path during the flight, much to the dismay of one trying to leap near the back of a stage without obliterating scenery, props, or corps members! The motion described above will consist of a series of flights following trajectories above straight lines on the floor, with brief moments of contact with the floor during which the direction of motion is changed.

FIGURE 3-5   Moving in a curved path, which requires a force from the floor toward the center of curvature. The lean of the body shown in this photo allows for that force, much as the banking of a curved road allows cars to follow the turn without skidding.

## Stopping Horizontal Motion

A dancer moving linearly across the floor may wish to stop moving, disposing of all linear momentum. Again, the floor is the source of the decelerating (slowing) force when the body leans back so that the center of gravity is to the rear of the support, allowing the floor to exert a retarding force to slow the forward motion. One often sees a traveling combination ending with a jump to one landing foot. The landing on the extended front foot allows for a forward force against the floor, which results in the appropriate retarding force of the floor against the body.

*Motions Without Turns*

## Vertical Jumps

Movements common to all forms of dance, and in fact many other athletic activities, involve vertical jumps—movements in which the body spends some time in the air with no contact with the floor or ground, returning to the surface close to the departure point. Unlike a simple object such as a ball, the human body can change its configuration during the time in the air, giving rise to some interesting phenomena.

Most tall and long-footed dancers have experienced difficulty when asked to perform rapid vertical jumps. These jumps must be executed in the rhythm of the music, with reasonable elevation, and, particularly in ballet, with pointed feet. Sometimes these requirements are physically incompatible, and compromises must be made.

All jumps involve vertical accelerations and forces. Because gravity acts vertically downward on our bodies at all times, we can remain motionless only if there is a vertical supporting force equal to our weight. In order to jump off the ground vertically we need to exert a force downward against the floor *greater* than our weight, for long enough to achieve the vertical upward velocity desired. Although small vertical velocities may be achieved with the feet alone, most jumps require an acceleration from bent legs—a *plié* position.

The height of a jump depends on the downward vertical force exerted against the floor and the length of time or vertical distance through which that force is exerted. Suppose $R$ is the ratio between the vertical force exerted against the floor and the dancer's weight. (If the two are equal, $R = 1$; if the dancer exerts a vertical force of twice his weight, $R = 2$.) If the vertical distance over which the force is exerted is $d$, the height of the jump is given by

$$H = d\,(R - 1).$$

If a *plié* lowers the center of gravity one foot, then a vertical force of double one's weight will allow for a jump in which the center of gravity rises one foot above the equilibrium value. Of course, the assumption that the force is constant during the upward acceleration is a crude one, but if we mean the *average* force exerted during that time, the general results are valid and illuminating. Studies have shown, however, that *too* deep a *plié* decreases the average force that can be exerted, and there is

FIGURE 3 6 Benjamin Pierce performs a vertical jump.

actually some sacrifice in the height of the resulting jump. Of course, what is "too deep" depends on an individual dancer's strength. And the movement leading to the jump is important also; a jump from a *plié* at rest is less effective than a jump moving into and out of the *plié* in one smooth motion in which the vertical force against the floor is already established before the rising movement starts.

An important consideration in jumps involves the timing, determined by the rhythm of the music. Here the length of time the body is in the air depends *only* on the height of the jump, not on the body size or weight, since the acceleration due to gravity is the same for all weights. (See appendix A for a mathematical analysis of vertical jumps.) But the relationship is not linear. That is, for the time in the air to double, the height of the jump must more than double. Some examples may be useful.

Let the height of a jump mean the vertical distance the body's center of gravity rises from the moment of take-off to the peak of the jump, and call that height $H$. Let $T$ be the total time during

TABLE 3-1  Height versus time in a vertical jump.

| T (seconds) | 1/4 | 1/3 | 1/2 | 1 |
|---|---|---|---|---|
| H | 3 in | 5.5 in | 1 ft | 4 ft |

which there is no contact with the floor. Table 3–1 shows how much the height of the jump changes for small changes in the timing. That strong dependence of the height of the jump on small changes in the time aloft is one of the main reasons dancers are acutely sensitive to slight changes in tempo. A decrease in tempo of just 10 percent means a dancer would have to jump 20 percent higher to stay with the music, a difficult feat if the dancer is close to the limit of jump height. Of course the message to the dancer is to slow the timing during the *plié*, since the motion in the air cannot be changed once contact with the ground is lost.

Now suppose the choreography and tempo of the music call for vertical jumps that must be accomplished in one-third second. The height of such a jump will be about 5 inches for *any* body. Suppose all dancers are told to point their feet during the jump. Those with small feet can do that because the height of the jump is sufficient to allow for a pointed foot with clearance above the floor. But the long-footed dancer is simply out of luck! There is no way he or she can point the foot in the time allowed. Increasing the height of the jump in order to provide clearance above the floor extends the time of the jump, and the movement is no longer performed in rhythm. (More will be said about the effects of body size in chapter 6.)

## Traveling Jumps

So far in this chapter we have looked at horizontal motions (accelerations from rest, slowing from forward motion, and traveling in a curved path) and vertical motions (jumps) separately. It is true that the two motions are separable for the purposes of physical analysis—horizontal forces produce horizontal accelerations and vertical forces produce vertical accelerations. But there are connections. Jumps combined with horizontal motions (such as *grands jetés*) produce trajectories, or paths of motion in space, that have certain well-known properties. It is also true that there are connections between vertical forces at the floor and the horizontal forces that result from friction. These friction forces would not exist without some vertical force pressing the foot against the floor.

What is the shape of the trajectory in the air for the *grand jeté*, and what control does the dancer have over that trajectory? Once the body loses contact with the floor the center of gravity will follow a parabolic trajectory that is *totally determined* by the conditions of motion at the beginning of the trajectory. (The parabola is the particular shape of the curved path in space.) Although the dancer may change the shape and configuration of the body in flight (which can produce certain illusions), there is nothing the dancer can do to change the trajectory of the center of gravity until contact is reestablished with the floor. The trajectory will be a combination of a constant horizontal velocity and the vertical motion associated with a jump—a motion rising with decreasing speed, an instant with no vertical motion, followed by an accelerating downward motion. The time of flight is still given by table 3–1, which was developed for purely vertical motion.

It is true that a jump with horizontal motion can be higher than a vertical jump because of the transfer of some of the horizontal momentum to vertical momentum. (An extreme case of this transfer is seen in a pole vaulter who uses the flexible fiberglass pole to maximize the transfer of horizontal momentum to vertical.)

## The *Grand Jeté* "Floating" Illusion

An interesting illusion can be created by changing the body configuration during flight. One sometimes sees an impressive *grand jeté* in which the dancer seems to defy gravity by floating horizontally near the peak of the jump for a brief time before beginning the descent, rather than following the curved trajectory. This effect is partly due to the simple fact that the vertical motion of the body is rapid at the beginning and end of the jump, but slow near the peak as the vertical speed slows to zero and reverses for descent. In fact, half of the total time the body is in the air is spent within one-quarter of the height to the peak. That is, if the center of gravity rises 2 feet during the *grand jeté*, the total time in the air is about 0.7 second, half of which (0.35 second), is spent within 6 inches of the peak. But the dancer can manipulate the body in such a way that this floating illusion is even stronger.

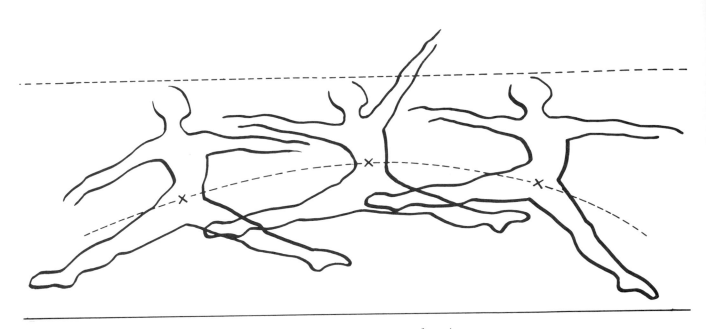

FIGURE 3-7 The *grand jeté* "floating" illusion, in which the center of gravity follows a parabolic trajectory, but moves its position in the body as the configuration of the body changes.

FIGURE 3-8 Sean Lavery's *grand jeté*, illustrating the illusion described in the accompanying analysis and shown in the diagram in figure 3-7.

Although the center of gravity follows a curved trajectory that is determined by the conditions of the initial jump from the floor, the position of the center of gravity *relative to the body* can be changed. Suppose the center of gravity when the dancer first leaps is in the abdominal area, when the legs and arms are rather low. When the center of gravity has risen partway through its curved trajectory, the arms and legs are raised, causing the center of gravity to move up in the body, perhaps to the stomach or above. If the timing is right, the center of gravity will continue to rise to the peak of the curved path, then begin to fall, while the torso and head of the body actually move horizontally. (See diagram in figure 3–7.) Since the eye of the observer is likely to follow the head and torso, an illusion is created that the dancer is actually floating horizontally for a few brief moments! A necessary component of the body movement that produces this illusion, then, is the raising of the legs, ideally to a "split," at the peak of the leap. Such a split is often seen in an impressive *grand jeté*, but it is now seen not only as an added stylistic flair unrelated to the jump itself, but as a component of the motion contributing directly to this illusion of "floating." But the split must be timed to coincide with the peak of the curved path of the body's center of gravity in order to produce the smoothest appearance of horizontal motion. The sequence of four instants in the *grand jeté* demonstrated by Sean in figure 3–8 shows many of these characteristics.

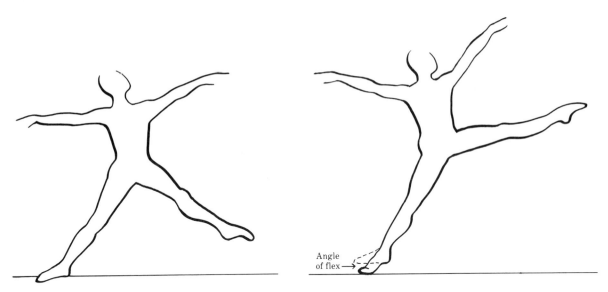

Angle
of flex →

FIGURE 3-9  Push-off for a *grand jeté,* with exaggerated turn-out.

## The Effect of Turn-out on Traveling Jumps

Should a traveling jump such as a *grand jeté* be performed with the feet and legs turned out? The accepted aesthetic quality for essentially all *ballet* movements includes turn-out. A *grand jeté* to the side, however, represents one movement in which another important quality, the height of the jump, is sacrificed if the normally expected degree of turn-out is maintained. Compromise is clearly necessary, in which a choreographer's or teacher's judgment determines the quality most important for the immediate purpose.

Consider two extremes. In the first case the *grand jeté* is performed *en face,* moving directly to the dancer's left, with complete turn-out, so that the right foot is pointed directly right as the push-off for the *grand jeté* to the left occurs. In the other extreme, the body is turned toward the direction of motion and turn-out is totally sacrificed, so that the *glissade* becomes a running step to the left, with both feet pointed to the left, in the direction of motion. (See figures 3-9 and 3-10.)

The jump will be significantly stronger and higher in the latter case. The reason involves the angle through which the push-off foot moves while the ankle extends, allowing the foot to exert

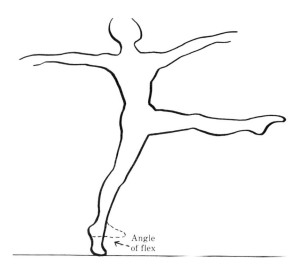

Angle
of flex

FIGURE 3-10   Push-off for a *grand jeté* without turn-out.

the force against the floor that results in an upward acceleration of the body. If the right foot is turned out, it is already partially extended at the beginning of the rise of the heel off the floor. The calf muscles then extend the foot, resulting in the force through the foot against the floor. As shown in the diagrams in figure 3-9, the angle through which the force can be exerted is thus less than 90°, from a partially extended position to a fully extended angle. However, when the foot is pointing in the direction of movement, it is flexed to an acute angle with the leg at the beginning of the jump, and thus can ideally extend through a change of significantly more than 90° to the fully extended position. When the force is exerted through a larger angle of travel of the foot, more energy is contributed to the jump. (The two approaches to the *jeté* are demonstrated by Sean in figure 3-11.)

Of course, in the dance movement described, one would never observe either extreme discussed here; there is always some degree of compromise. But it is true that the human body is constructed such that our feet generally point in the direction of movement. This body configuration contributes to the effective use of the muscles in accomplishing the purpose of running or jumping.

FIGURE 3–11 Sean Lavery pushing off for a *grand jeté* with and without turn-out, as shown in the diagram in Figure 3-9.

## Landings from Jumps

Now let us consider the deceleration, or sudden decrease in downward speed, that occurs as the body lands from a jump. Of course, the foot will decelerate more rapidly than other parts of the body because it has no other springy body part beneath it to cushion its fall or extend its deceleration. The torso must decrease its downward velocity to zero from the free-fall velocity just before landing, but the bending of the legs allows this velocity change to occur over a sizable distance (perhaps 1 foot) and an associated time of about one-quarter second. The landing foot and lower leg, however, must lose the same velocity of fall in a much shorter distance. Suppose the sole of a shoe and the padding of flesh between the skin and the bony structure of the foot can compress a total of 0.1 inch. For a jump in which the center of gravity has risen 2 feet, the downward velocity just before landing is about 11 feet per second. If that velocity changes to zero in a distance of 0.1 inch, the deceleration is about 240 times the acceleration due to gravity, or 240 $g$! Although the total mass of the foot that must be decelerated is small, that deceleration can be potentially harmful to the foot.

Dancers are sometimes called upon to fall to the floor, rather than simply to land from a jump. Again the decelerating forces can be large, depending on what part of the body strikes the ground first, and with what vertical velocity. If the hands are used to break a fall, the same analysis as applied above for the feet can be used to analyze the effect on the hands. Of course, if much of the weight of the falling body is subsequently borne by the hands, that continued stress can cause problems and even injury. In any case, the nature of the floor can have a major impact on how the body reacts to landings or falls.

## Dance Floors—Elasticity and Friction

Note that the horizontal accelerations discussed earlier depend on friction between the feet and the floor. And the effectiveness of vertical jumps is thought to depend on the quality of the floor—the amount of "spring" in the floor. Floors that are too rigid may also produce injuries. Thus some discussion of the characteristics of dance floors seems appropriate here.

Both the elastic properties and the surface friction of dance floors are often inadequate for the demands dancers place upon the floors. First let us consider the vertical elastic property of a floor, which is important for a safe landing. Elasticity involves both large scale "springiness" and small-scale "rubberiness." Does a springy floor aid in the jumping process as a diving board would, or does it allow higher jumps only because of the psychological effect of an anticipated softer landing? Actually, the magnitude of vertical motion in a springy floor is rather small— less than an inch—while the vertical displacement of the body's center of gravity during the push-off for a jump is at least a foot.

This implies that the contribution of the floor to the magnitude of vertical velocity at the end of the push-off is rather small.

Let us return to the deceleration experienced by the foot upon descent and landing from a jump. If the padding provided by the shoe and the sole of the foot allows a compression of 0.1 inch, then the deceleration upon landing is about 240 times the acceleration due to gravity. But if the floor adds additional vertical motion of 1 inch, the deceleration is only about one-tenth as great. Thus the seemingly insignificant "give" in the floor results in a large decrease in the potentially dangerous deceleration of the body.

This principle is very evident in some easily observed situations. The air bags used by high jumpers and pole vaulters for their landings extend the time and vertical distance over which the free-fall velocity may be decreased to zero. An automobile bumper with some spring to it will cause and sustain less damage than a stiff one. Closer to home, there is less discomfort when one trips and falls if the landing is made on the padded buttocks than on the unpadded head!

Now, what benefit is gained from the use of the linoleum or rubber-like stage floors commonly used for dance? The most important properties are probably the controlled uniformity and sound-deadening capability. Many stages have holes, grooves, slippery spots, and other problems that can be covered by a portable dance floor. And the sound of a hard shoe surface (as on the toe of a *pointe* shoe) striking a floor can be decreased substantially by even a small amount of small-scale elasticity. But it is also true that this small scale "give" in a floor increases the area of contact between the toe of a *pointe* shoe and the floor. On a hard surface the curved toe will ride on the floor with only a very small part of the convex surface making contact. That small part will, of course, have an extremely large pressure due to the body weight, and will wear rapidly. A slightly elastic floor surface will allow the shoe to sink into the surface a small amount, allowing a larger area of contact. Not only should this be easier on the shoe, but dancers claim they benefit from a greater "feel" of the floor.

Now we return to a traveling jump such as the *grand jeté* and a dancer's common concern for the potentially slippery floor. Is rosin on the floor always the appropriate solution? What are the principles involved in the frictional properties of floors?

Friction involves the properties of surfaces, both chemical and mechanical. Both chemical adhesion between surfaces and microscopic roughness contribute to a frictional force that acts in a direction along the interface between the surfaces. For many pairs of interacting surfaces the magnitude of the friction force is proportional to the perpendicular force pressing the two surfaces together. The constant of proportionality is called the "coefficient of friction."

Rosin is used on a floor to increase friction. Whether a dancer needs a change in linear horizontal motion or a rotational acceleration, the floor must be able to supply the horizontal forces that provide for such accelerations. The perpendicular (vertical) force is equal to the person's weight if there are no vertical accelerations, so the only way to increase friction is to change the nature of the surfaces.

Many dance movements involve sliding on the floor, or rotating on a pivoting supporting foot. Too much friction will inhibit these movements, which may include *glissades* and *assemblés*, in addition to all types of *pirouettes*. One characteristic of rosin is that it has a large static coefficient of friction and a significantly smaller dynamic coefficient. That is, if the foot is stationary on the floor, a large horizontal frictional force is possible, but if the foot is moving, that force is substantially smaller. That difference is very useful to a dancer, who needs the horizontal force only when the foot is not moving against the floor. (That difference is also the reason rosin is used on bows for stringed instruments, for which a stick-slip-stick-slip process is responsible for the resonant oscillation produced by the bow on the string.)

Why don't modern dancers, who perform many of the same sorts of movements as ballet dancers, use rosin? Modern dance is usually performed with bare feet. Since the skin is usually somewhat moist (particularly when the body is exercising), the characteristics of the surfaces in contact are different than when dry. A small amount of moisture makes surfaces in contact less slippery; too much moisture reverses that effect, since there can now be a film of water between the surfaces. The normal skin moisture is appropriate for the movements of a modern dancer, whereas rosin adds more friction than the bare feet can withstand, giving rise to blisters or worse. Ballet dancers often use a little water on the floor or the shoes to provide a degree of friction similar to that of moist bare feet.

## A Final Step

A dancer performing linear movements—vertical, horizontal, or a combination—must understand and control the forces exerted against the floor. These forces are responsible for the accelerations, or changes in the state of motion. Horizontal acceleration from rest requires a horizontal force against the floor. This force can arise from a shift in the center of supporting force relative to the center of gravity of the body, or from an acceleration of part of the body that results in a force against the floor.

Motion in a horizontal curved path requires an acceleration, in this case because of the change in *direction* of the velocity. That acceleration requires a horizontal force, which can come only from a lean toward the center of curvature, as in a banked curve on a road. The faster the motion, or the tighter the turn, the greater the lean from vertical. Friction against the floor is often the limiting factor in establishing how fast or tight the curved path can be.

Horizontal motion can be stopped only if there is a horizontal force against the floor in the direction of motion (resulting in a force from the floor on the body in a direction such as to oppose the motion). A landing from a jump would have to be made with the center of gravity behind the landing foot in order to allow the body to coast to a stop in a stable position.

Vertical jumps require vertical forces against the floor that must be adjusted to produce the height required and the time in the air determined by the rhythm of the music. The relationship between height and duration is fixed by nature, and is independent of body size. It takes a jump four times as high to last twice as long.

In-flight trajectories, involving combined vertical and horizontal motions, always have a parabolic shape for the path of the center of gravity. Nothing a dancer does after take-off from the floor can change the trajectory of the center of gravity. The horizontal component of motion in the trajectory is always a straight line while the body is in the air. The vertical component of motion is identical to a vertical jump in place. The illusion of "floating," or temporarily stopping the downward acceleration at the peak of the jump, is accomplished by shifting the position of the center of gravity in the body, so that the torso and head move only horizontally for a short time near the peak of the jump while the center of gravity continues its parabolic curved trajectory.

The vertical impulse that can be produced for a traveling jump depends on the range of motion of the foot around the ankle pivot. In some cases that range of motion is limited when turnout is maintained, and the height of a jump is sacrificed.

Both elastic and frictional properties of dance floors are important for dancers, the former for vertical motions, and the latter for horizontal accelerations. Elasticity contributes little to the vertical impulse in a jump, but it does allow a softer landing that decreases the potential for injury. Rosin is used to increase friction of the feet against the floor because it tends to be "sticky" when there is *no* motion, but allows motion more easily once the feet are moving on the floor. Thus *glissades* and *pirouettes* are possible at the same time that the friction allowing for rapid accelerations or decelerations is present.

Dancers are well aware of the dangers involved in large movements on stage. Probably every dancer has experienced the embarrassment of a fall. When one recognizes the forces between the feet and the floor that are necessary in order to carry out the movements observed, it may be a wonder that these movements are possible at all! Just the inward lean of the body during a circular movement around the stage invites a slip and fall. And the forces required for the high leaps, particularly in the landings that are most likely to produce injury, can be enormous. But there is no way of avoiding these forces if dancers are to display the full range of the movements expected of them. The audience, and the art of dance, is well served by these efforts on the part of dancers!

# 4

# Pirouettes

Turning movements are common in all forms of dance. One of the most common turns is the *pirouette*, or rotation of the body over one supporting foot on the floor. There are many types and styles of *pirouettes*, from a low turn on bent leg or a pencil turn in modern dance, to *attitude* or *arabesque* turns, *en dehors* or *en dedans* turns, or the impressive multiple *fouetté* turns or *grandes pirouettes* often seen in the classical ballet repertoire. The various turns have both common aspects and uniquely different characteristics and problems.

Brief descriptions of these turns will be useful. An *en dedans* turn is any *pirouette* toward the supporting leg (a right turn on the right supporting leg, for instance). An *en dehors* turn is *away* from the supporting leg. In the normal *pirouette* position in ballet, the supporting leg is straight and almost vertical, and the gesture leg is raised to the side with the foot at the knee of the supporting leg (sometimes called a *retiré* position). An *arabesque* turn is usually an *en dedans pirouette* with the leg extended to the rear in *arabesque* position. *Attitude* turns can be *en dedans* or *en dehors* (more difficult and less common), *en*

FIGURE 4–1   The New York City Ballet performs George Balanchine's *Serenade.*

FIGURE 4-2  Benjamin Pierce performs an *en dedans* turn in a style typically seen in modern dance.

*avant* or *derrière*. A *grande pirouette* is a turn with the leg extended horizontally to the side (*à la seconde*). *Fouetté* turns are repeated *pirouettes en dehors* with the gesture leg extended away from the body during a part of each turn when the dancer is facing the audience.

## Torque and Rotational Momentum in a *Pirouette*

If a body is initially at rest, and a short time later is moving as a whole, some interaction with the world outside of the body is necessary. In the same way that a body at rest is caused to move linearly in some direction by a force acting on it, a body is caused to rotate by a torque applied to it. In general, a body can be caused to move as a whole in some direction *and* rotate simultaneously. But in order to avoid that complex situation, this chapter will deal with pure rotations, or turns that leave the horizontal position of the body's center of gravity unchanged.

Pirouettes

A torque can be thought of as a kind of force that causes a rotation, as the hand turning a screwdriver, or two hands turning a T-shaped wrench to tighten bolts on a car wheel. A torque is actually a combination of at least two forces acting on a body in different directions, with some distance between the lines along which the forces are acting. Widely separated forces acting on a body are more effective in producing rotations than forces acting close together. For instance, thin-handled screwdrivers and short-handled wrenches are more difficult to use to tighten bolts than large-handled tools.

Consider a dancer starting a *pirouette* from a fourth-position preparation, with one foot some distance behind the other on the floor. When the turn is started, the dancer pushes sideways in opposite directions with the two feet, as shown in figure 4–3. The result of the forces of the floor acting on the feet (associated with the forces exerted by the feet against the floor) is to create a torque that starts the body rotating. If the feet are very close together, as in a fifth-position preparation with one foot immediately behind the other and pointed in the opposite direction, the torque is smaller; it is harder to initiate the turn, just as it is harder to tighten the bolt with a small-handled wrench. Requiring even more force, and therefore more difficult, is a turn in which the torque is exerted by just the supporting foot while it is still flat on the floor. In that case, the front of the foot pushes one sideways direction, and the back of the foot the other. (Experiments have shown that, as expected because of the direction of necessary twist of the foot, this "single-foot torque" applies only to *pirouettes en dedans* [see note 2].) In any case, the possibility of exerting any torque at all effectively ends when the supporting foot rises onto *pointe* or *demi-pointe*, and the physical dimensions of the contact area become very small.

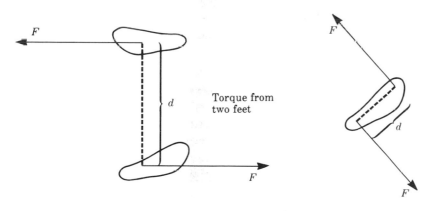

FIGURE 4–3 Force couples and torques between the feet and the floor, which produce the turning motion for *pirouettes*.

Torque from two feet

Torque from one foot

Pirouettes

FIGURE 4-4  Narrow and wide fourth position preparations for a *pirouette en debors*. The wide fourth, with the larger distance between the forces, requires less horizontal force between the feet and the floor to produce the same torque.

Rotational momentum is a "quantity" of rotational motion. The total rotational momentum $L$ of a body can change only if there is an external torque acting on the body. There is no way that changes in body position alone—changes in the configuration of mass within the rotating system—can change the total magnitude of $L$. It is sometimes claimed that "spotting" the head one more time can squeeze an extra turn out of a multiple *pirouette*. ("Spotting" is keeping the head fixed in direction while the remainder of the body turns, then rotating the head quickly around to face the original direction again.) But rotating the head relative to the rest of the body does not change the total rotational momentum of the body as a whole, and hence cannot contribute any extra turning motion. One may feel as if the extra turn is there, but the additional rotation of the head only gives the *appearance* of a full additional turn. Then why do dancers spot? Apparently spotting of the head prevents dizziness by providing a fixed focus for the eyes and a nonrotating head for part of the movement.

What determines how much rotational momentum a dancer can acquire in a *pirouette*? The dancer's feet push sideways against the floor, in opposite directions, in order to produce the torque that starts the turn. The total rotational momentum acquired in that process is determined by the size of the torque exerted on the body *and* by the length of time that torque is applied. Suppose a dancer initiating a *pirouette* begins to push against the floor in a way described above, so that a turning motion begins. If the orientation of the body changes quickly, so that it is impossible to continue exerting those forces, then the final rotational momentum will be limited. But if there is some way of storing the rotational momentum acquired during the push so that the body can remain in its initial orientation, then the length of time the torque can be exerted on the body can be increased, resulting in a greater accumulated total rotational momentum. How does the dancer accomplish this storing of rotational momentum? One technique is often seen, particularly when *pirouettes* are performed from fifth position for which the distance between the lines of action of the forces at the feet, and hence the resulting torque, is small. The arms are observed to "wind up," or start rotating before the rest of the body does. Those arms are thus storing rotational momentum that is eventually transferred back to the body as a whole, allowing for a greater rate of turn.

Although a greater turn rate can be achieved by means of the "wind-up," dancers are usually admonished not to employ it, or at least to minimize it. This is an example in which use of the physical principle that makes a movement easier is counterproductive in achieving the desired aesthetic image, since most teachers, choreographers, and dancers feel that the appearance of the turn is compromised by the wind up. Maximizing the rate of turn is not considered as important as other visible aspects of the movement.

## Controlling Rotational Velocity

The feeling and appearance of a *pirouette* is directly related to the turn rate. How is that turn rate related to the total rotational momentum? The rotational momentum $L$ is greater if the rate of turn (number of revolutions per second) is greater *or* if the mass of the body is distributed farther from the rotation axis. So for a given rate of turn, a dancer's $L$ is greater when the legs and arms are extended to the side than when they are close to the body, and for a constant body configuration, $L$ is greater the more rapid the turn.

The important thing about rotational momentum is that it is a quantity that remains constant when no torques act on the body. In that case, a change in the distance of body mass from the rotation axis will produce the opposite change in the rate of turn. That is, if the arms or legs are brought closer to the body, then the rate of turn will *increase*, assuming there is little friction at the floor that would tend to decrease the total $L$.

Suppose a skater is rotating with little friction between the skates and the ice, so that $L$ is about constant. When the arms and legs are brought closer to the body, bringing the mass closer to the rotation axis, the rate of turn must increase. A similar change is seen in a dancer performing a *pirouette* with leg in *retiré* (foot at the knee of the supporting leg) and arms extended to the front in balletic first position. When the body position is changed so that the lifted leg descends and is brought closer to the axis of rotation, and the arms are brought closer to the body, the rate of turn increases. Of course, dancers experience more friction between the foot and the floor than skaters, so $L$ will actually be slowly decreasing. But as the distribution of body mass changes, the expected decrease in turn rate can be partially offset, making the turn appear to continue at a constant rate longer than if the body were kept in a constant position. That phenomenon is quite evident in Mikhail Baryshnikov's eleven-turn *pirouette* in the movie *White Nights*.

When learning *pirouettes*, one sometimes hears the instruction to "go up and then turn." Since the rotational momentum $L$ is constant after the accelerating torque ceases, this instruction seems impossible. However, the arms are often extended during the accelerating phase of the turn, so that the rate of turn is not too large while $L$ is increasing to its maximum. Then, when the arms are brought in closer to the body, the turn rate increases, thus creating the illusion of turning only after rising onto the supporting foot. In the case of the *arabesque* turn or the *grande pirouette*, the body remains extended, so the rate of turn never becomes very large. (But that turn rate again increases near the end of the turn if the working leg is finally brought in to the normal *pirouette* position for the last few rapid turns.)

What slows the *pirouette*, limiting the number of turns possible? When a dancer is *en pointe*, the area of supporting contact with the floor is very small. We have seen how this affects conditions of balance. It is also true that there is less retarding torque for *pirouettes* performed *en pointe*. The perpendicular force holding the foot and the floor together is still just the dancer's weight, so the total horizontal friction force is expected to be the same. But the torque resulting from those forces depends on the distance from their line of action to the rotation axis. If the area of support is small, the friction forces act very close to the axis of rotation, so the resulting retarding torque is small. (A quantitative study of the slowing of *pirouettes* was published in 1993.[1])

When the turn is to be stopped, the foot (or feet) returns flat to the floor, allowing the retarding friction to increase, and the arms are extended, which slows the rotational velocity for the rotational momentum remaining. Coordinating these two actions of the body allows the turn to end in the desired orientation.

## Different Types of *Pirouettes*

Let us look at some of the differences between types of turns. The examples are all from the classical ballet vocabulary, but the results may be generalized to other forms of turns around a vertical axis on one supporting foot. Recall the *en dehors* and *en dedans pirouettes*, *arabesque* and *attitude* turns, *grandes pirouettes*, and *fouetté* turns described earlier.

Experiments have shown that the total rotational momentum is significantly less for *pirouettes en pointe* than for those on *demi pointe*, least for *pirouettes en dehors*, and greatest (about 30 percent larger) for *arabesque* turns.[2] The latter is interesting in that the rate of turn is faster (more than double) for the *pirouette en dehors* than for the *arabesque* turn. Clearly, the distance of body mass from the rotation axis makes the difference; it is substantially greater for the *arabesque* turn with extended leg. So even though a greater $L$ is achieved for such a turn, the turn rate is small because of the extended body position.

The same experiments mentioned above also showed that the rotation of the head during the turn ("spotting") occupies about half of the total time of the turn for a *pirouette en dehors*. For the slower turns, the head often just turns with the rest of the body.

FIGURE 4-5 "Drooping" leg in an *arabesque* turn.

## The *Arabesque* Turn

An *arabesque* turn in classical ballet, an *en dedans pirouette* with one leg extended to the back of the dancer, is a beautiful movement when performed well. But there is a common error one can observe in students learning the movement or in dancers lacking the requisite proficiency. The prevalence of this error has an interesting physical reason behind it.

FIGURE 4-6 Sequence of five consecutive instants in an arabesque turn, demonstrating the "drooping" leg problem. The gesture leg oscillates down and up once during the complete turn shown.

The *arabesque* turn requires exerting a torque with the two feet on the floor, then lifting the push-off leg into a horizontal position to the rear, where it is not visible to the dancer. After the leg reaches the horizontal position there is a strong tendency for it to drop back down, as in a *grand battement derrière*, or kicking movement to the rear. (See figure 4–5.) When the leg is fully extended horizontally, it represents a substantial part of the body mass extended far from the rotation axis, which makes the rate of turn small for the magnitude of $L$ that resulted from the initial torque. When the leg drops, its mass is not as far from the axis of rotation, so the turn rate increases, making the turn seem easier, faster, and more satisfying. The drooping leg, since it is behind the body, is not easily seen by the dancer (except in the wall mirror often present in class).

An interesting phenomenon now occurs. Since the turn rate has increased, there is an increased centrifugal force tending to throw the leg away from the axis of rotation out toward the horizontal again! The resulting decreased turn rate then allows the leg again to descend, and the process may repeat. So a dancer may experience an oscillation of the leg up to the horizontal, down, then up again, possibly repeated for a multiple *arabesque* turn. (See figure 4–6.) In fact, such an oscillation can be observed in dancers who do not concentrate on keeping the leg fixed in the *arabesque* position, as detected by proprioceptive senses—the internal senses the mind uses to determine body positions without visual cues.

One may ask if this oscillating leg syndrome is bad; perhaps the choreographer intends such a movement. The traditional *arabesque* turn in ballet, which is a common and impressive movement, is done ideally with the gesture leg fixed in a horizontal position. Choreographers do sometimes depart from the ideal for artistic reasons, and similar turns in other styles of dance may depart in specific details from the classical ballet model.

Lisa de Ribère performed the *arabesque* turn with the "drooping leg" for the camera in order to illustrate the problem. The resulting sequence of photographs is shown in figure 4-6.

At what frequency might the gesture leg be oscillating up and down? The problem is not a simple one, because the centrifugal effect tending to throw the leg out depends on the rate of turn of the body, but that turn rate itself depends on the angle the gesture leg makes with the vertical. It often happens in physics that parts of a problem can be analyzed individually, but when the parts are interdependent, they cannot be solved separately. The results of an analysis described in appendix G show that for a typical body shape and turn rate, the leg's oscillation frequency is very close to the rotation frequency. That is, for a rotation rate of one full turn in about 2 seconds, the leg may oscillate up and down at the same rate; that is, once each revolution. This "resonance" between the two frequencies may make it particularly difficult to overcome the oscillating leg problem, since the natural frequency of that oscillation is synchronized with the rotation! The good *arabesque* position would occur when the body is facing one side, with the *arabesque* line facing the audience, then occur again when the body returns to that orientation. In between, the dancer rotates rapidly when the leg is lower. But a perceptive audience will realize that the leg has drooped during the rotation, thereby violating the normally accepted standard of an *arabesque* turn.

## The *Grande Pirouette*

Another interesting effect occurs in a *grande pirouette*, and also in other turns with a straight extended gesture leg, such as the *arabesque* turn described earlier. Since the body position for the *grande pirouette* is identical to a stationary pose often seen—the body *en face* with the gesture leg horizontal to the

FIGURE 4-7 Sean in second position, stationary and turning. The condition for balance is slightly different in the two cases, with the supporting leg closer to vertical when the body is rotating, in the view on the right.

side *à la seconde*—one might wonder if the condition for balance is the same whether the body is rotating or not. The physical analysis of the condition for balance for a static body is straightforward, involving the masses, lengths, and positions of the various body segments. As shown in the photograph in figure 4-7a, the supporting leg is not quite vertical because of the amount of weight that is extended to one side. For typical body segment masses and lengths, one can calculate the angle the supporting leg makes with the vertical. This angle is about 4.5° for a male dancer. (The *grande pirouette* is more often performed in ballet by male dancers.)

Now suppose the body is rotating about a vertical axis through the supporting foot, as in figure 4-7b. If the supporting leg again makes an angle of 4.5°, will the body be in balance while rotating? Strangely enough, no! The analysis is complicated, and is described in appendix H. Briefly, it involves the following: since the body position for the *grande pirouette* is not bilaterally symmetric (the right and left sides of the body have different configurations), the rotational momentum must precess around the vertical axis, as with a spinning top that is wobbling. That precession of *L*, necessary for a balanced turn, requires an angle between the supporting leg and the vertical that is less than the static 4.5°—in fact, about 3.5° for the same data used for the static equilibrium. Although this difference in balance angle is small, and variations in the performance of the movements may be large enough to mask the effect, the photographs of Sean in figure 4-7 do seem to show a slight difference in angle. Good dancers must be sensitive to very small shifts in position in order to achieve the remarkable feats of balance sometimes observed. Without a sensitivity to this shift in balance when the body is rotating, it is difficult to carry out the movement well. The magnitude of that challenge is one reason the movement is impressive and rarely performed well.

## *Fouetté* Turns

*Fouetté* turns are repeated *pirouettes* that begin as a normal *pirouette en dehors* but include a movement that allows the rotational momentum lost to friction to be regained once each revolution. Properly done *fouetté* turns are an impressive "tour de force" in a ballerina's vocabulary. One of the best-known examples in standard classical choreography is the thirty-two continuous *fouetté* turns by the Black Swan in Act III of *Swan Lake*.

This turn is one of the few continuing turns, a fact that immediately suggests the question "How does the dancer maintain balance and replace rotational momentum lost because of friction for an extended time?" The turn itself is a series of repeated *pirouettes* with a pause in the turn after each full rotation. (The sequence of photographs in figure 4-8 shows Lisa in various stages of a *fouetté* turn. A clockwise path through the six pictures shows the stages of the movement in proper order, and may be continued for the repeated turns.) While the body is turning, it is in a normal *pirouette* position, with the arms forming a circle to the front and the gesture leg to the side with the foot at the knee of the supporting leg. When the torso and head are facing front, the gesture leg is extended to the front, the arms start to open, and the supporting leg is bent slightly, with the heel down. As the gesture leg moves from front to side it absorbs the rotational momentum of the turn while the torso, head, and arms remain facing the audience.

When the gesture leg is brought in to the knee of the supporting leg again, and the dancer rises onto straight leg and pointed foot, the whole body again turns through a complete revolution, since the rotational momentum now resides in the

1

6

2

5

4

3

FIGURE 4-8 Lisa de Ribère performing *fouetté* turns. The sequence should be viewed clockwise through the six frames, which are then repeated. Note that the body rotates very little while the leg has most of the rotational momentum in views 2, 3, and 4. Then the body turns rapidly in 5 and 6 while the leg is held in a position close to the body where it has less rotational inertia.

Pirouettes

entire rotating body. The period of time during which the dancer's body is not rotating (less than one-half second) provides an opportunity for regaining balance and exerting some torque against the floor with the flat supporting foot, thus regaining any momentum lost by friction.

What characteristics of this movement can be changed by a choreographer or a dancer without destroying the movement itself? Which characteristics are dictated by physical principles, and which are determined by aesthetic considerations? An important aspect of the turn is the motion of the gesture leg from front to side while the body is temporarily stationary. In fact, the Russian style of the *fouetté* turn involves thrusting the leg directly to the side, which of course slows the rotation because of the increase in distance of body mass from the rotation axis, but does not allow the torso, head, and arms to stop briefly. In both styles, it is necessary to have the gesture leg extended as far from the rotation axis of the body as possible in order for it to absorb the total rotational momentum of the turn without acquiring too large a rotation rate itself, or, in the Russian style, to maximize the distance of the leg's mass from the axis of rotation so as to slow the body's turn rate as much as possible during that phase of the movement.

Quantitative calculations have been made on the basis of data on weights and dimensions of body segments for an average female dancer, and a model of body positions for a good *fouetté* turn. Suppose a dancer is doing a normal *pirouette* at a rotation rate of two revolutions per second. When the body is facing front, the gesture leg is extended forward and begins rotating to the side while the remainder of the body remains nonrotating. If the total rotational momentum $L$ remains approximately constant during this entire turning cycle, then the turn rate is small when a significant mass of the body is far from the rotation axis. The calculations described in appendix I show that the rotation rate of the extended leg is only about one-half revolution per second when the rest of the body is not rotating. The movement of the leg from front to side (one-quarter turn) thus takes about one-half second, long enough for the dancer to regain balance and exert some torque with the supporting foot. This stationary phase of the total movement takes about half of the total time for a complete cycle of the motion, while the full-turn rotation of the body takes place in the remaining half.

## Repeated *Pirouettes*

A similar analysis applies to another repetitive turn—repeated *pirouettes* from fifth position. These are often turns *en dehors* (away from the supporting leg), with the body descending off *pointe* or *demi-pointe* into *demi-plié*, with both feet down once each revolution when the body is *en face*. Again, there must be a mechanism for the body to exert a torque against the floor in order to regain the small amount of rotational momentum lost to friction during the turn. This torque can most effectively be exerted by the feet against the floor if the body is temporarily stationary. The means of stopping the body is similar to that for the *fouetté* turn, but in this case the *arms* rather than the gesture leg rotate while the body stops. When the body reaches a position facing front, the lead arm and then the trailing arm rotate toward the turn, thus temporarily absorbing the rotational momentum and allowing the feet to perform their torque-exerting function. When the body returns to the *pirouette* position, the arms transfer the rotational momentum back to the body as a whole.

Since in this movement the arms, which are lighter and shorter than a leg, are less effective than the gesture leg in the *fouetté* turn, the effect is less noticeable, and the repeated turns do seem to be more continuous. But the fundamental mechanical process is the same.

Another example of a turn in which the same effect can be detected is the *grande pirouette* discussed earlier in this chapter. This turn usually includes a return to flat supporting foot and *demi-plié* once each revolution. In this case some torque is exerted by the supporting foot against the floor during the time the foot is flat rather than on *pointe* or *demi-pointe*. Again, this torque can be exerted more effectively if most of the body is temporarily slowed, if not stopped, in its rotation. The gesture leg does swing a small amount in the horizontal plane during that *en face* moment, and the arms may help some, too. The effect is less pronounced than for the previously described turns, but a good dancer will adjust body position somewhat to make the movement as smooth as possible by controlling where the rotational momentum resides during different phases of the turn.

## A Final Turn

All of the turns discussed in this chapter have common characteristics involving the preparation, the mechanisms for developing the torque to initiate or maintain the turn, and the control of the body's mass distribution to determine the rate of turn. Some repeated turns involve, in addition, transfers of rotational momentum from one part of the body to another.

All turning movements require a torque to create the rotational momentum needed. For solo *pirouettes*, the torque comes from a force couple exerted by the feet against the floor. The larger the distance between the lines of action of the two forces making up the force couple, the greater the torque. Thus, a *pirouette* preparation position in which the feet are spread far apart allows the forces at the feet to be more effective in producing the accelerating torque. *Pirouettes* from fifth position, as well as *pirouettes* in which the torque comes largely from just one foot in contact with the floor, are more difficult for the same reason. *Pirouettes en dehors* are initiated by torques exerted only while *both* feet are on the ground; the torque for *en dedans* turns can involve some contribution from the supporting foot after the push-off foot has left the floor.

In starting a turn, it is usually effective, although not always aesthetically acceptable, to rotate the arms in the direction of the turn while the torque is being exerted against the floor. The arms thereby absorb much of the rotational momentum while the body is in a position that makes possible the effective use of the feet for exerting torque.

Controlling the turn rate after rising onto *pointe* or *demi-pointe* requires controlling the distribution of body mass relative to the rotation axis. The farther the body mass is from the axis, the slower the rate of turn. This fact explains why a *grande pirouette* is made more rapid by bringing the arms and legs close to the body. It also explains the mechanism for a *pirouette en dedans* when started with a *dégagé à la seconde*, which delays the turn of the torso at the beginning.

*Arabesque* turns are slower because of the amount of body mass that is far from the axis of rotation. And they are often flawed by a gesture leg that oscillates up and down during the turn. This oscillation is a natural phenomenon that can, in fact, have the same period of oscillation as the period of rotation, making the problem particularly insidious. The placement of the body and the strength with which the gesture leg is held in position are extremely important in maintaining the *arabesque* line during this turn.

The *grande pirouette* requires a balance position slightly different than the position of balance for the same position without the rotation. The effect of the turn is to require the supporting leg to lean a bit less away from the vertical than it does for the nonrotating case.

*Fouetté* turns require a temporary pause in the rotation once each revolution when the dancer is facing front. That pause is made possible by transferring rotational momentum from the whole body to the gesture leg, which rotates from front to side while the rest of the body remains facing front. That rotation of the gesture leg is therefore an important characteristic of the *fouetté* turn. Repeated *pirouettes* from fifth position involve a more subtle transfer of momentum, which is based on the same principle. In this case the rotational momentum is transferred to the arms, which temporarily rotate relative to the rest of the body while the dancer is facing front.

To what extent are dancers aware of the physical principles that govern the way rotations occur? As in many other cases, but particularly for the subtleties of rotational motion, dancers have learned by experience, instruction, trial and error, and observing others, just how to perform the movements. It is a wonder that they achieve the desired results so effectively, in ways that unconsciously use these mechanical principles that are usually applied to wheels, gyroscopes, and planets.

## Notes

1. K. Laws and L. Fulkerson, "The Slowing of *Pirouettes,*" *Kinesiology and Medicine for Dance* 15, no. 1 (1992-1993): 72-80.
2. K. Laws, "An Analysis of Turns in Dance," *Dance Research Journal* 11, nos. 1, 2 (1978-1979): 12-19.

# 5

# *Turns in the Air*

Leaps in the air are an impressive aspect of any form of dance, but leaps or jumps with simultaneous rotations involve an additional dimension. *Tours jetés* and *demi-fouettés* are jumps with 180° rotations around a vertical axis while the dancer is in the air, initiated from a traveling start and a jump from one foot. *Sauts de basques* and turning *assemblés* are usually jumps with at least one full rotation in the air, again starting with a jump from one foot. *Tours en l'air* are turns in the air (usually two) around a vertical axis, starting with a jump from two feet. The challenges to the dancer are to control the amount of rotation gained by contact with the floor, then to control the rotation in the air after leaving the floor, and finally to get rid of the turning motion upon landing.

The *tour jeté* can be a sharp and impressive movement in classical ballet, and has counterparts in other forms of dance in which turns are combined with leaps. The *tour jeté* is particularly effective if the body appears to rise up from the floor, *then* turn through a half revolution to face the opposite direction, and then return back to earth, landing on the foot opposite the

FIGURE 5–1  Sean Lavery airborne in a scene from George Balanchine's *Stars and Stripes*.

take-off foot. How is that illusion accomplished? And why is it an illusion? Why is it easier to accomplish the rotation for a *demi-fouetté*, for which the landing is on the same foot as the take-off? How does one create the opposite illusion in the *saut de basque*, in which the body appears to *pause* in its rotation at the peak of the leap? What characteristics of the movement are important in achieving the rate of turn necessary for these turning leaps, especially in those cases in which a double turn is called for? How is the body coordinated so as to achieve the turn in the double *tour en l'air* so common in male variations in classical ballet? Also important is the question of how the rotation in each of these movements is *ended* without the dancer coasting past the desired final position and orientation.

Each of these movements, like the *pirouettes* discussed in the last chapter, involves a rotation of all or part of the body around an axis. There are similarities and differences in the analyses that provide insights into the physical principles involved in these turning movements. Rotational momentum is again the important quantity, since it must be constant during the time the body is in the air when no forces or torques (other than the uniform vertical force of gravity) can act on the body.

## The *Demi-fouetté*

The *demi-fouetté* is a jump with a half turn. Take-off is from the right foot, and the left leg kicks to the front as the right foot leaves the floor. The left leg remains oriented toward the direction of motion while the rest of the body flips through its 180° rotation, landing then on the right leg, facing the direction from which the dancer came. Very little torque needs to be exerted against the floor, because the gesture leg, in which most of the rotational inertia resides, maintains its direction in space. Only the torso, head, supporting leg, and arms must revolve around the axis of rotation during the turn in the air.

In fact, suppose this movement is carried out with *no* torque against the floor. In this case the total rotational momentum of the body remains zero, still allowing part of the body to rotate in one direction while another part rotates in the opposite direction. The torso, head, and arms can rotate a full half turn to the right, while the gesture leg revolves to the left. The movement of the extended gesture leg is small, since it is far from the axis of rotation and its rotational inertia is large. An approximation to a good *demi-fouetté* can be carried out in this way. (This technique of turning with zero rotational momentum is a part of the complicated movements a cat executes when righting itself in the air after being dropped upside down.)

## The *Tour jeté*

The *tour jeté* is also a jump with a 180° turn around a vertical axis, the dancer landing on the foot opposite to the take-off foot. In this case the dancer faces the direction of motion when he takes off from his right foot, and kicks a straight left leg into the air in front of him. After take-off, his right leg moves up to meet the left, and he does a half turn to the right, landing on the left leg, right leg to the rear, and facing in the direction from which he came. The sequence of photographs in figure 5–2 shows Sean Lavery in consecutive stages of the *tour jeté* described.

Ballet dancers being taught this movement often hear an instruction something like, "Square your shoulders and hips! The turn is most brilliant when you rise straight up and then start to turn right at the peak of the jump!" When laws of physics are applied to such a model of the movement, one quickly concludes that such a feat would involve a violation of conservation of rotational momentum. (See appendix B.) But if this movement is observed as it is performed by an accomplished dancer, one does indeed see the body apparently turning in the air after contact with the ground has ended. How is this illusion created, and how can a dancer maximize the effectiveness of the illusion? Rhonda Ryman has provided some insights into this movement.[1] The analysis is complex, and best carried out mathematically, but a qualitative description is presented here.

If the body is undergoing a net rotation while in the air, there clearly must be some rotational momentum associated with this turn in the air. But there can be no rotational momentum unless there has been some torque acting on the body. Once the body has lost contact with the floor, there is no longer a source of torque, so whatever rotational momentum existed at the moment of take-off is maintained throughout the flight phase of the movement. The torque must be exerted against the floor before take-off, so that the turning motion is established. But when the foot leaves the floor, the body has a large rotational inertia (see appendix B), meaning that the body's mass is distributed far from the axis of rotation. The left foot is extended to the front,

FIGURE 5-2 Sean Lavery performing a *tour jeté*. Note that the rotation has begun while the legs are approaching each other, and stops when the rotational inertia is large in the final *arabesque* position aloft.

the right foot has just left the floor to the rear, and the arms are rising in front of the body. Since the rotational momentum is equal to the product of the rotational inertia and the turning rate, the rotation rate can be quite small when the body mass is spread far from the axis of rotation. But there is some rotation, as seen in the second view of Sean's *tour jeté* in figure 5-2, in which his body has turned somewhat as he approaches the peak of the jump.

At the peak of the jump, the legs cross close to each other along the axis of rotation, and the arms simultaneously come together overhead, also close to the axis of rotation. Thus, the rotational inertia is decreased substantially at that time, and the rate of rotation increases accordingly. The appearance to an observer is that the body has suddenly acquired the turning motion at the peak of the jump. Upon landing, the arms open to

the side and the right leg extends to the rear in *arabesque*, thus increasing the rotational inertia again, and slowing the turn rate.

This analysis provides some clues to the dancer as to how to maximize the illusion of turning sharply at the peak of the jump. The legs must cross close to each other and the arms must come overhead *at the time the jump has reached its peak* in order to accomplish the decrease in rotational inertia at that moment, with the associated increase in turn rate. The body must approach as closely as possible a straight-line configuration so that the mass is close to the longitudinal rotation axis. Note from the photograph of the *tour jeté* (figure 5-2) that the axis is inclined somewhat from the vertical at the peak of the jump when the rotation is occurring.

It is important to note that these characteristics of the *tour jeté* that are necessary for the illusion of "flipping" around at the peak of the jump are also consistent with the aesthetic requirements of a properly performed *tour jeté* according to traditional classical ballet standards. But the reasons for those characteristics are now seen to be not only aesthetic, but also based on compatibility with physical principles that *must* apply to the movement.

There is another style of *tour jeté* that emphasizes an aspect of the movement different from the illusion of flipping over in the air described above. It also applies a different physical principle. In this case the gesture leg kicks to the front, and the rest of the body turns *while* that leg is far from the axis of rotation and therefore has a large rotational inertia. That is, the first part of this movement is identical to the *demi-fouetté* described earlier. But after the torso, head, and arms have rotated through 180°, the legs are reversed through a scissors motion so that the landing is again to the foot opposite to the take-off foot. In this form of the *tour jeté* the body flips to an *arabesque* position in the air very early, and then the legs reverse position. The impression is that the upper body floats down gracefully after the quick turning motion is completed. So whereas the first type of *tour jeté* depended upon a change in the body's configuration, allowing a rapid rotation of the whole body near the peak of the jump, the latter type involves allowing all the body except the free leg to rotate in one direction while the free leg remains far from the rotation axis, then reversing the legs late in the movement.

74

## The *Saut de basque*

Let us look now at the *saut de basque*, another jumping turn. (Hannah Wiley has carried out a comprehensive study of the *saut de basque*.[2]) The right foot is again the push-off foot, and the left leg kicks forward in the direction of motion. In this movement, however, the body initially turns one quarter turn so that the left leg, still extended in the direction of motion, is now extended to the side of the body in second position. (The arms are also extended to the sides at that time.) As the dancer approaches a landing on the left foot, his body rotates to the right to a position facing the audience, with the right leg in a *coupé* position in front of the ankle of the left leg. This movement is illustrated in the sequence of photographs of Sean in figure 5–3.

The jump in this movement involves the same principles discussed in chapter 3. The height of the jump is enhanced by the transfer of horizontal linear momentum to the vertical direction. That transfer must be controlled so that the linear motion is stopped at the end of the movement, or some motion is retained if the following movement continues traveling. The height of the jump must, of course, be sufficient to accomplish the turning motion while the dancer is in the air, although the landing must be made slightly *before* the body faces the audience so that the supporting foot can exert the torque against the floor for a time long enough to decrease the rotational momentum back to zero.

FIGURE 5–3   Sean performing a *saut de basque* jumping turn. Note that the body turns little until the right leg comes in to the *retiré* position, which decreases the total rotational inertia.

As we have seen before, once the body leaves the floor there is no more torque, and the rotational momentum must be a constant until landing. The torque must be exerted by the take-off foot before it leaves the floor. (There is no possibility of a torque from *both* feet, since the two feet are not in contact with the floor at the same time in the running steps preceding the jump.) Note the importance of the full foot being in contact with the floor during the jump so that the torque can be as large as possible. When the heel leaves the floor, very little torque can be exerted by the small area of the foot remaining in contact.

When the legs and arms are extended, the rotational inertia is large, and the body seems to pause in its rotation, a characteristic of a well-executed *saut de basque*. As the left leg is brought down in preparation for the landing, and the arms and right leg are brought in closer to the body, the rotational inertia decreases significantly, and the body turns rapidly. The landing, with the retarding torque exerted by the supporting foot, completes the *saut de basque* turn. Again it is important to lower the left heel to the floor so that the full length of the foot is involved in the retarding torque.

Note that *too much* momentum would make it difficult to stop the turn at the end, since there would be only one foot on the floor at that time that could exert the retarding torque against the floor. The timing of the pause with arms and leg extended is crucially important. If they remain extended for too long a time, the faster rotation that occurs after they are retracted will not occur before the landing. If the arms and leg are brought in too soon, there will be too much rotation with the smaller rotational inertia, and the movement will not end with the dancer facing the audience.

The double *saut de basque* is usually performed without the pause with extended arms and left leg. The reason is clear. In order to accomplish two full turns (actually one and three-quarters turns), the rotational inertia must be kept as small as possible so that the rotation rate is sufficiently large to accomplish the rotational movement during the time in the air. The right leg may be in a *retiré* or *coupé* position during the turn, so that when the left leg is in *plié* after landing, the right leg does not drop to the floor. Figure 5-4 shows Sean near the peak of a double *saut de basque*, in which his body is much closer to the axis of rotation as he rotates than is the case with the "spread" position near the peak of the single turn.

FIGURE 5-4   In a double *saut de basque* turn, the rotational inertia must be kept small throughout the movement in order for the necessary rate of turn to be maintained. The position shown here, rather than the extended position seen in figure 5-3, is maintained through most of the double turn.

## The Turning *Assemblé*

The turning *assemblé* is similar to the *saut de basque*, except that the legs are straight and close to vertical, and the landing is made to both feet. The arms are usually overhead during the turn. In this case the rotational inertia is quite small, since the body mass is as close to the axis of rotation as is possible. The turn can be quite rapid, and double turns are easier than the double *saut de basque*.

One aspect of the turning *assemblé* is worth noting. If the rotational inertia is small at the *beginning* of the movement, while the take-off foot is exerting the torque against the floor, it will be difficult for a dancer to acquire sufficient rotational momentum. The body will rotate away from its initial orientation too rapidly to allow the torque to have its effect in producing the rotational momentum. It will be difficult to accomplish the double turn during the time in the air, because the turn rate cannot be significantly increased after take-off. If the rotational inertia is larger at the beginning, then it can be decreased after take-off, thereby speeding the turn.

Although the left leg may extend somewhat during the initial phase, the arms are most important. The arms should extend and begin rotating in the direction of the turn before contact with the floor is lost, thereby absorbing much of the rotational momentum generated by the torque at the foot before the body rotates very far. The arms then move to the overhead position, and the rotational momentum resides in the whole body as it turns. The arms moving directly from side to overhead, rather than moving down in front and then overhead, reinforces the quick decrease in rotational inertia, making the turn more effective.

If the landing is in fifth position, the feet are close together, and exerting torque to *stop* the turn is difficult. It is again necessary to land before the turn is completed, allowing the body to slow to a stop in the desired direction.

## The *Tour en l' air*

The double *tour en l'air* is most commonly performed with the body compacted as close to the vertical axis of rotation as possible, in order to maximize the rotational velocity while the body is in the air. The legs are straight and vertical, and the arms are close in front of the body. The head spots twice during the double turn. Although the preparation for a *tour en l'air* normally has the feet close to fifth position, many dancers find that the torque against the floor is too small (because of the small distance between the lines along which the forces act), and separating the feet somewhat in fourth or second position (separated front to back or side to side, respectively) makes the turn easier.

Either of two aspects of the *tour en l'air* may be emphasized when performing this movement. The horizontal forces exerted by the feet against the floor produce the torque that results in the rotational momentum for the turn. The vertical force exerted by the feet pushing against the floor produces the height of the jump that allows the body time to rotate. Emphasizing the horizontal forces will produce a rapid turn, while jumping higher and sacrificing horizontal force will produce a slower turn with more time in which to complete two full revolutions.

Of course, the horizontal forces exerted by the feet against the floor must be a force *couple*, involving two equal and opposite forces, in order to produce a rotation with no horizontal acceleration away from the initial position. A common error is to distort the body somewhat (buttocks pushed back, for instance) in the *plié* immediately preceding the jump. The effect is to throw the body off balance with the net horizontal force that results from such a distortion at the time of push-off.

Any movement that ends in a static position must involve some forces or torques that remove the momentum associated with the movement. When the *tour en l'air* is completed to a static position, the feet must have sufficient friction with the floor to exert the retarding torque necessary. Thus again the body should return to the floor before completion of the turn so that it may coast to a stop facing the audience. If the rotational inertia is increased (by extending the arms, for instance) as the body coasts to a stop, the rotation rate decreases so that there is little turning after landing. The decreased turn rate at the end makes the direction the body is facing when landing less critical than if the body were continuing its rapid rotation.

## A Final Leap

All of the turns described in this chapter have involved the torques, rotational speeds, and rotational momenta also used in dealing with *pirouettes*. The jump has added some complications because of the combination of two kinds of motion. But the power of the physical analyses is particularly evident as these more complicated and spectacular movements succumb to careful treatment.

An effective *tour jeté* involves an illusion that requires controlling the rotation rate while in the air. The legs and arms must be brought as close as possible to the straight line around which the body is rotating at the time the peak of the jump is reached. This allows the rotation rate to increase drastically at that time, creating the illusion of flipping around at the peak of the movement. The *demi-fouetté*, while similar to the *tour jeté*, requires less rotational momentum, and hence less torque, since the gesture leg maintains its orientation in space rather than revolving. A second type of *tour jeté* is effectively a *demi-fouetté* followed by a reversal of the legs so that the landing is to the foot opposite to the take-off foot.

The *saut de basque* involves a similar control of the turn rate in the air, but this time the body is *extended* at the peak of the jump so as to create the illusion of *pausing* briefly in the turn. Since the take-off and landing both involve just one foot, the accelerating and slowing torques require the full foot to be on the floor, maximizing the effectiveness of the feet in exerting the required torques. The double *saut de basque* turn eliminates the "pause," because the body must remain compact in order for the dancer to maintain the turn rate required for two full turns before landing.

The turning *assemblé* and the *tour en l'air* both require careful control of the rotational inertia of the body. It must be as large as feasible before take-off so that the turn is relatively slow while torque is being exerted against the floor. After take-off, the rotational inertia is decreased to provide a rapid turn rate. The arms, in addition to contributing to a large rotational inertia when they are extended at the beginning of the movement, also absorb some of the initial rotational momentum by rotating relative to the body at the beginning of the turn. When it is in the air, the whole body shares the total rotational momentum. In both of these turns, the landing must be made before the turn is completed, so that the body can coast to its final orientation while slowing to a stop. The slowing can result only from the retarding torque exerted by the feet against the floor.

A low, rapid turn is created by emphasizing the horizontal force couple exerted by the feet against the floor, while a high jump without so fast a turn results from emphasizing the vertical force. The proper emphasis will, of course, depend on the rhythm and the character of the choreography.

One important way to control the timing of the body rotation is to control how the arms move. Their rotation can be isolated from that of the rest of the body, and if they are far from the axis of rotation they can carry a substantial rotational momentum. Thus the coordination of arms is an important aspect of both the style and the mechanics of the turns discussed in this chapter.

Turns in styles of dance other than classical ballet will also involve the control of the important mechanical parameters of the movement—rotational speed, body position and configuration, and the appropriate accelerating and decelerating torques against the floor. The physical analyses of this chapter can be applied to any turns for which the characteristics are sufficiently specifiable and understood.

When any of these rotations with jumps is observed, two movements are happening at once. Dancers are challenged to coordinate the two movements so that, for instance, a landing does indeed occur as the desired amount of total rotation has been accomplished. Unlike linear velocity, which can be changed only by means of forces from outside the body, rotational velocity can be changed by controlling the body's distribution of mass relative to the rotation axis, even when in the air where there is no contact with an agency of force. This fact provides an additional degree of freedom for dancers, but also makes the control physically more complex. This combination of freedom and necessary control contributes to the impact of these rotations in the air.

## Notes

1. R. Ryman, "Classical Ballet Technique: Separating Fact from Fiction," *York Dance Review* 5 (1976): 16. Also, "A Kinematic and Descriptive Analysis of Selected Classical Ballet Skills" (Master's thesis, York University, 1976).
2. Hannah Wiley, "Laws of Motion Controlling Dance Movement: A Qualitative and Kinematic Analysis of *Saut de Basque*" (Master's thesis, New York University School of Education, Health, Nursing, and Arts Professions, 1981).

# 6

# *The Effects of Body Size*

A tall man has a distinct advantage when partnering tall women, but height can be a disadvantage for other types of movement. *Adagio* movements may appear smoother when performed by a tall person, but *allegro* movements require considerably more strength than the same movements, to the same music, performed by shorter dancers.

Vertical jumps with "beats" of the legs, or scissoring movements that separate the legs and then bring them together again (*entrechats quatre, entrechats six,* etc.) represent a type of movement for which an analysis of the effects of body size is most intriguing. We will also look at horizontal accelerations, *pirouettes,* and some specific examples of *adagio* movements.

Suppose Sean Lavery, who is over six feet tall, has an understudy who is 5′ 3″ tall who is attempting the same choreography. How much more difficult are jumps and *entrechats* for tall people than for short people, and why? Why is it that tall dancers have more difficulty getting the feet pointed or clearing the

FIGURE 6-1  George Balanchine with a young Judy Fugate.

ground sufficiently to perform the required movements? How much more strength does the tall dancer require to perform the same movements as the shorter dancer in the same tempo? What special problems do horizontal accelerations and *pirouettes* present for the larger dancer?

Dance teachers are particularly aware of differences between children and adults in the performance of dance movement. Although adults often have better-developed muscles, coordination, and understanding, one often notices children performing certain types of movements more easily. Dance students undergoing a growth spurt in their early teen years usually experience a temporary loss of grace and body coordination. And choreographers are often aware that they must have different expectations of large and small dancers in terms of line, tempo of music, and general style of movement.

What are the physical bases of these effects of body size on the execution of dance movements? It is well known that accelerating a large mass requires a larger force than changing the velocity of a small mass at the same rate. But some of the more subtle "scaling" problems are not so obvious.

## Height of a Vertical Jump

First let us consider vertical jumps. Much of this analysis applies to any jumps, whether in ballet, modern dance, or even non-dancing activities. Often in dance choreography there is vertical motion *and* beats with the legs while the dancer is in the air. We will deal with the vertical motion first and then the beats. In chapter 3 the relationship between the time in the air and the height of a jump was discussed. We saw that the height of a jump depends strongly on the duration of the jump as determined by the music tempo, making dancers particularly sensitive to that tempo.

One implication of the relationship between time and height for a jump is that dancers of different sizes must jump the same absolute height off the floor in order to perform to the same tempo. If the tempo is slow, the shorter dancer may not be able to jump sufficiently high to "fill" the music, which leads to an apparent jerkiness. But there is another aspect of the jump that creates a *disadvantage* for the tall dancer. Part of an observer's impression of the height of a jump depends on its height *relative to the dancer's height*. That is, for a jump taking one-half second

FIGURE 6-2  A short and a tall dancer jumping to a height about the same proportion of their own height will be in the air different lengths of time. Here the daughter of one author, Virginia, substitutes for Sean Lavery's "understudy," and arrives at the floor before Sean, who jumped higher.

in the air, the jump height of about one foot may be one-quarter of body height for a short dancer, but only one-sixth for a tall dancer. Such a jump is just not as impressive looking for the tall dancer. Again, there is nothing the tall dancer can do to extend his jump height without taking a longer time and lagging behind the music.

Figure 6-2 shows Sean Lavery with a substitute understudy (the daughter of one of the authors) who is close to the 5' 3" referred to earlier. In this case the taller Sean jumps to about the same proportion of his height as the shorter Virginia (in the second photo), but clearly, as shown in the last view, he arrives back at the floor later than the shorter dancer.

Now let's consider the strength required to support or move a larger body. We've all noticed how a skinny-legged spider easily carries more than its own weight, or a flea is able to jump many times its own height, while the fat legs of an elephant hardly do more than support the animal itself. The reason can be

*The Effects of Body Size*

understood if we imagine two geometrically similar animals, such as a rat and a mouse, one of which has exactly the same shape (the same body proportions) as the other but is twice as large in each linear dimension. The volume, and hence the mass, of the body is proportional to the third power of the linear dimension; the rat thus has a weight eight times that of the mouse. But the cross sectional area of the legs supporting the body depends on only the second power of the linear dimension, so that the rat has only four times the leg area of the mouse. Thus, the rat is supporting eight times the weight on four times the area, resulting in double the stress or pressure on the leg structure.

Excess stress or pressure on the body is responsible for injuries, which is one reason small people suffer fewer injuries. Of course, young people of any size have more flexibility in bones and tissues, which contributes to their resilience and affords some protection from injury.

An important effect of size is the force a muscle can exert, which is roughly proportional to the cross-sectional area of the total packet of fibers in a particular muscle. If our rat has muscles twice the linear size of the mouse's, the muscles would have four times the cross sectional area and could exert four times the force. But if the mass to be accelerated is eight times as great, the rat is going to have more difficulty in its movements and must exert more muscular effort to move at the same rate as the mouse.

How do these scaling principles apply to dancers? Suppose a young male dancer is 5′ 3″ tall, while Sean is just over 6′ (15 percent taller). Further, suppose their bodies are identically shaped (same proportions). Sean will weigh about 52 percent more than Shorty, and will have muscles 32 percent stronger (because they are 32 percent greater in cross-sectional area). Thus, in order to jump to a height of one foot, taking one-half second, Sean must exert 15 percent more muscular effort. Alternatively, in order to jump to a height of about one-fifth of his own height (a one-foot jump for Shorty), Sean must jump about 1.2 feet and exert 32 percent more muscular effort than the shorter dancer.

Consider the energy required for this movement, which is directly related to the number of calories burned in the process of moving the body. The physical work done in a vertical jump is the product of the weight and the height, and thus is 52 percent more for Sean than for Shorty. If each dancer jumps *to the same proportion of his own height*, Sean expends about 75 percent more energy! These relationships apply in varying degrees to all kinds of movement, and dancers of different sizes have learned to adjust to the expectations placed upon them. But fatigue does depend to some extent on the total expenditure of energy, and large dancers sometimes have to expend *much* larger magnitudes of energy in order to carry out similar moves.

## Entrechats

Now let us consider the beats with the legs that Sean must perform while in the air during his jump. These beats are oscillating rotations of the leg around a horizontal axis through the hip joint. A torque is required at the hip in order to produce the rotational acceleration (see appendix B). In order for *entrechats* to be accomplished in the same tempo by both Sean and Shorty, and with the same angular amplitude (perhaps oscillating through an arc of 10°), the rotational accelerations of the legs will be the same for both of them. As shown in appendix B, the torque required is proportional to the rotational inertia, which depends not only on the mass, but on the square of the distance of the mass from the rotation axis. (The contributions from the individual parts of the leg at their distances from the hip must be added.) Thus the rotational inertia of a leg is proportional to the fifth power of its linear size. Sean's leg has 101 percent more rotational inertia than Shorty's (about double), and Sean must exert *double the torque* to produce the same rotational acceleration, and hence the same leg motion in the same tempo!

Other factors make the problem less severe. Sean's muscles, which are 32 percent larger in cross-sectional area, can exert 32 percent more force for the same "effort." And the structure of the joint, including the distance from the center of the joint to the point of muscle attachment to the bone, is also bigger in Sean. This allows a particular muscle force to produce more torque. The final result is that Sean must still exert 32 percent more muscular "effort" to perform beats at the same rate as his smaller counterpart!

How about the energy expended doing *entrechats*? Since the angular movement is assumed to be the same for the different bodies, the energy required is proportional to the torque. Thus Sean is expending energy at about *double* the rate as Shorty!

## Horizontal Accelerations and Body Size

Suppose a dancer must undergo a quick horizontal acceleration away from his initial position. As we have seen in chapter 3, this acceleration is proportional to the horizontal friction force between the foot and the floor, and inversely proportional to the body's mass. Since the friction force is proportional to the weight, there is no advantage or disadvantage associated with size in realizing sufficient nonslipping friction force to accomplish a particular linear acceleration.

But how does the dancer achieve the off-balance condition necessary for a horizontal force and acceleration? These techniques, discussed in chapter 3, do involve slower processes for larger dancers. For instance, the toppling of the body from a vertical configuration to one of increasing angle with the vertical makes it possible to exert an increasing horizontal accelerating force against the floor. But the rate of topple is slower in direct proportion to the linear size. So it will take longer for a tall dancer to "topple" to a sufficient angle to exert the required horizontal accelerating force against the floor.

## Body Size and *Pirouettes*

Let us look at the effects of body size on a *pirouette en dehors*. In performing this movement does a tall dancer experience a disadvantage or an advantage compared to a shorter person?

The rotational inertia of a body around any axis of rotation depends on the fifth power of the linear size of the body (assuming the same shape for bodies of different sizes). So Sean's rotational inertia around a vertical axis is double that of Shorty. Sean can exert 32 percent more force with his muscles (which are that much fatter than Shorty's). The horizontal forces of the feet against the floor, which produce the force couple that initiates the *pirouette*, are thus 32 percent greater for Sean. However, the same body position will produce a 15 percent larger distance between front and back feet in the preparatory position, so the accelerating torque will be 52 percent greater for Sean than for Shorty. But we're then left with a rotational acceleration 32 percent less for Sean than for Shorty, or else Sean must exert 32 percent more muscular effort than Shorty in order to perform the *pirouettes* at the same rate.

Now the frictional force at the floor is a problem. When the shoe is not moving against the floor, the horizontal force between the two surfaces can be as great as $F = CW$, where $C$ is the coefficient of static friction and $W$ is the body weight. (Note that the force does not depend on the surface area of contact.) Thus, for a given coefficient of friction, the friction force can be as great as 52 percent greater for Sean than for Shorty. The greater spread of feet in the preparatory position means that the torque can be as much as 75 percent greater for Sean. But in order to produce the same rotational acceleration as Shorty, Sean must exert a torque that is 101 percent greater. Thus, the larger dancer may require a larger coefficient of friction—requiring more rosin, for instance—to perform *pirouettes* at the same rate as a smaller dancer. Slipping of the feet at the beginning of a *pirouette* can be more of a problem for Sean than for Shorty.

## *Adagio* Movements

Most of the effects of size discussed here result in disadvantages for the large dancer. It is true, however, that slow movements sometimes look more graceful and smooth when performed by taller people.

One reason for the smoothness of movement possible for taller dancers involves the slower accelerations that result from the muscular effort of a large person. When Sean exerts 90 percent of his strength in a particular movement, his body responds with a corresponding acceleration. Shorty, to produce movement at the same rate, will exert perhaps 50 percent of his strength. It is probably easier to control the body smoothly when the exertion required is close to zero or close to maximum, and hardest halfway between where sizable variations in exerted strength are possible either direction from the magnitude required for the movement. Thus, Shorty will have more difficulty moving smoothly at the slow tempo that requires less of his strength.

## Effects of Body Shape

In these analyses of scaling factors, it was assumed that bodies of different sizes had the *same shape* (or body proportions). It is probably true, however, that a dancer 15 percent taller than another is less than 15 percent larger in the lateral dimensions. Many of these analyses would have to be changed slightly if the assumption of same shape were invalid. Some of the disadvantages of height would be less severe. However, it is interesting to note that if the larger person were relatively less broad in the lateral dimensions (i.e., if he were more slender in shape), one would have to assume also that the cross-sectional area of the muscles was larger by *less than* the second power of the linear dimension. Some of the compensating factors would disappear, and the disadvantage of size would remain!

## A Final Comparison

These results are summarized in table 6-1, which lists the various body and movement characteristics, and the percentage by which each is greater for Sean, a $6'\frac{1}{2}''$ dancer, than for Shorty, a $5'3''$ dancer with exactly the same shape, or body proportions, as Sean.

What are the disadvantages and advantages for a tall dancer as compared to a short one, then? First, for the same time in the air as determined by the tempo of the music, the taller person may have trouble completing the movement in the allotted time with pointed feet, since the height of the jump is the same, independent of body shape or size. Second, the appearance of elevation in a jump depends somewhat on the height of the jump *relative*

TABLE 6-1   Percentage by which certain body characteristics or movements are greater for a $6'\frac{1}{2}''$ dancer than for a $5'3''$ dancer.

| | |
|---|---|
| Height | 15% |
| Weight | 52% |
| Cross-sectional area of supporting legs | 32% |
| Cross-sectional area of muscles (and therefore muscle strength for a given "muscular effort") | 32% |
| Height of jump in a specific time interval | same |
| Energy required for jump to same height | 52% |
| Energy required for jump to same proportion of body height | 75% |
| Rotational inertia around any rotation axis | 101% |
| Torque required for a particular rotational acceleration around any axis | 101% |
| Muscular effort for a particular rotational acceleration—*entrechats* or *pirouettes* | 32% |

*to the height of the person*. The tall person does not appear to be jumping as high in the same length of time as the shorter person. But the energy required is significantly greater for the taller person.

The difficulty of executing beats with the legs while in the air is strongly dependent on body size. And because the inertia associated with the mass of a larger person determines the acceleration produced by a given force, horizontal accelerations are more difficult for larger dancers.

Since the torque required to produce a particular rate of turn is proportional to the body's rotational inertia, and the rotational inertia depends drastically on body size (*double* for a dancer 15 percent taller), the difficulty of executing smooth *pirouettes* is compounded with increasing size.

The one advantage that larger dancers have is a greater smoothness in performing *adagio* movements, because the movements require a greater proportion of their available strength. And some of the problems in other movements may be less severe because of the fact that taller dancers are generally not as much larger in lateral dimensions as in height.

What can the tall dancer do about some of these problems? Awareness of the reasons for the problems is the first step. Problems involving forces against the floor can be alleviated by the use of rosin on the floor or moisture on the shoes. The larger dancer must also learn to *anticipate* movements, starting to exert the necessary forces earlier than smaller dancers.

Sometimes larger dancers *are* observed carrying out quick movements. Recognizing the difficulty of that accomplishment, an observer may see ways in which this speed results only from the use of great strength, or may see ways in which adjustments are made that alleviate some of the difficulties. In companies with dancers of widely varying sizes, wise artistic directors are very conscious of the differences in movement styles appropriate to the different sizes. The analyses carried out here give a more quantitative idea of the magnitudes of those differences, showing that in some types of movement the effects of size are far greater than in other types.

# 7

# *The Image and Experience of the* Pas de Deux

## The Image of the *Pas de deux*

Interactions between performers in the arts vary. Visual artists usually work alone; the dramatic arts almost always involve performers interacting with one another. Music varies. Orchestra musicians must, of course, interact with a conductor and with one another, but musical interaction is perhaps most profound in jazz, where the sensitivity of each musician to the improvised music being created by others is the primary challenge and source of gratification for both the performer and the listener. It can be argued that music is a representation of life, but the connection is not so direct as in dance, in which people's bodies themselves are the medium of the art form.

FIGURE 7-1   Suzanne Farrell and Peter Martins in a scene from George Balanchine's *Allegro Brilliante*.

When dancers dance as partners, the appeal of the art form is strengthened by the interactions between people. Not only is the body moving, as it can do alone, but now it is interacting with another body in ways that imply some kind of social consciousness. The dance movements can be purely representations of human bodies moving while interacting physically with each other, or there can be representations of normal social interactions ranging from casual greeting to lovemaking, from helping to fighting, from desire to rejection. The images can be sexually neutral, with interactions that are totally symmetric between men and women, or, as is usually the case in classical ballet, interactions that are very distinct in the roles, purposes, styles, and movements of men and women. In any form, partnering in dance creates a compelling image because there is a basic human need to interact, both mentally and physically, with other people rather than to be totally isolated. The *pas de deux* in dance represents the interaction and touching between two people that elicits a strong response from the observer.

In the early days of formalized Western dance, partnering arose out of social dancing, which was not designed to be observed by audiences. "The steps . . . differed little from those of the era's ballroom dances; the theatrical form was simply more polished and studied" (Anderson 1986, 25).[1] Men and women began to dance together for the entertainment of others in the late seventeenth century, but at that time female roles were often played by men or boys.

The *pas de deux* as an important aspect of dance gained major impetus in the romantic era of ballet beginning with Marie Taglioni in the 1830s. As romantic ballets evolved during the nineteenth century, partners acted out romantic stories involving young princesses and their cavaliers. There were definite gender roles in which the woman was delicate and dependent and the man was strong, supportive, and controlling. The role of the man in helping to display his partner in the most effective way was established, as was the general format of these ballets. In fact, the primary role of the male dancer in ballet became, in the late nineteenth century, one of support for his partner. It took Nijinsky, near the turn of the century, to bring the role of men back to full dancing participation.

As dancers became more proficient and comfortable in the roles they were expected to fill, the level of difficulty of partnered movements expanded. The Russians introduced more athletic aspects of movement from the circus environment, giving rise to the big lifts that are often seen in the *pas de deux* of the twentieth century. It was discovered that if there was personal danger involved in the more athletic moves carried out by partners, the appeal to audiences was enhanced. A woman carried aloft at arm's length above her partner can create several images: perhaps the exhilaration of flying higher than one can alone, depending on another person's strength and good will, accepting the dangerous possibility of falling from that height, and demonstrating a skill that can only be vicariously appreciated by most observers.

Fantasy plays a major role in the *pas de deux* on several levels. First, most people do not have access to a partner who can carry out the sort of interactions displayed in partnered dance. The coordination necessary to do the more impressive moves seen in partnering—supported *pirouettes* and big lifts—is possible only for those who have the appropriate strength, body, and training. There is the fantasy of imagining oneself participating in those movements. But there is also the strong fantasy component of the *pas de deux* in classical ballet, the image of idealized romantic love. The guilt sometimes associated with enjoyment of erotica is removed; the observed interactions between dancers involve physical contact and the image of physical love, but without the suggestive or often overly sexual images that our society has defined as erotic. The *pas de deux* can represent a "clean" way to enjoy (vicariously) sexually oriented images.

Traditionally, the roles of men and women have been quite distinct; only recently have the expectations of these distinctions been suppressed. But the traditional roles were built around the known average anatomical differences between men and women. The average man is taller and heavier and can exert more muscular force than the average woman. The woman, on the other hand, is more likely to have greater flexibility, which allows her a greater range of line represented by body position. So if one partner is to provide lifting force or any other type of manipulating force on the body of the other, it is traditionally the man supporting the woman. If support allows a partner to display pleasing body line more effectively, it is the woman who traditionally is provided with that support.

One can speculate on other reasons for the way gender differentiation in the *pas de deux* evolved. In Western society, it has been traditional for men to "support" women in terms of labor and finances; such support carries over to the roles in partnering. But it is interesting to note that it is the male partner who must be most sensitive to the interpretation of the dance by his partner, responding to the subtleties of the woman's timing and style. Sensitivity and communication are characteristics attributed more often to women than to men. Returning to the art form of jazz, it is an intriguing fact that it is a performing art in which women are dramatically under-represented, although it is particularly demanding of artistic sensitivity to other people. Perhaps both jazz and partnered dance attract men who crave an outlet for their artistic sensitivity to a performing partner.

It is also true that traditional differentiations between male and female roles in society are changing. For instance, an increasing number of women are financially and emotionally providing support for themselves, families, and even men. And homosexuality is increasingly open and accepted. Dance, as a reflection of society, reflects those changes. *Pas de deux* movements are now seen in male/male, female/female, or reversed male/female combinations in addition to the traditional male/female combination, and the constraints of the traditional gender differentiation are often removed in all three formats. The partnered dances may have sexual connotations between partners of the same or opposite sex, or may involve interactions that have nothing to do with sex. In the purest form, such dances may involve only the aesthetics of the use of space by two interacting people. Thus, the basis for an audience's appreciation of partnered dance has been broadened.

But the average anatomical differences between men and women remain. The partnering movements seen in traditional classical ballet are compatible with those average differences, in that the man uses his strength to provide support and the woman uses her shape and flexibility to show a graceful line. When partnered dance removes the constraints of that traditional style, the movements are likely to be quite different, not involving the same sort of lifts and supported *pirouettes*. On the other hand, there are interactive movements that two strong men can carry out that might be difficult for a man and a woman. And society is increasingly open to noncompetitive physical interaction between men.

There are differences in partnering technique in different styles of dance that are quite apparent to the observer who is looking at dance with some depth. For instance, in ballroom

aloft, although she alone is responsible for the position she maintains when in the air.

But these physical aspects of the *pas de deux* are just the means to an end. The aim is to project an aesthetic image to the audience that represents a "conversation" between the two partners. Cynthia Harvey, who has had extensive experience in *pas de deux*, and is quoted specifically in this chapter, says, "When experiencing the *pas de deux* in performance, I often come away hoping that the audience was captivated by our 'conversation' as much as by the excitement of the physicality. It is so satisfying when the *pas de deux* goes well." Usually, by the time of the performance, the two dancers have developed a rapport that enables them to take a similar approach toward reaching the demanding goal of a good performance. People's approaches vary—it helps when dancers can verbalize to each other their intentions and how they wish to tell the story, especially as the story becomes clearer in time. Ideally, the two should have points of view that run along parallel lines. If they do not, then the conflicts or differences in their modes can still produce appealing final results.

Cynthia speaking: "When I have had bad experiences in partnering, the primary reasons have been mistrust, inexperience (in a particular role), and simply not seeing eye to eye with the person with whom I was dancing. Inexperience, either on my part or that of my partner, does not prove so disastrous if one of us has done the role previously, but when both of us are unsure, the result can often be frustrating, to say the least. It is desirable to have a partner who has danced his role before and who can share with me the knowledge and secrets he acquired from a previous partner. He can inform me of the musical innuendo that by now is comfortable for him and that will enable me to time my steps so that they coordinate with his. If the male partner has done the role before, he can suggest shortcuts and, in a sense, 'economical' energy-saving tips.

"I had one partner who was very experienced, having danced with a number of leading ladies. Instead of intimidating me with declarations of 'how Natalia did it,' he would simply state his suggestions as if they were obviously the best way. I listened; I was rather inexperienced and found him to be so absolutely right and such a great partner that he was able to eliminate any doubts that I might have had by virtue of the brilliant maneuvers he made. By contrast, I have also danced a *pas de deux* with a rather inexperienced gentleman. I made suggestions to enable a lift to work, based on my past experience, but he still wanted to try it his way first. Basically, it comes down to communication. Ultimately, a partnership flourishes in a highly communicative atmosphere, where give and take are a natural part of the creative process.

"When the experience has been bad, and the audience knows it, and when each of the two dancers involved is aware that it has been an 'off' performance, the feeling is one of complete and utter letdown. As dancers, after we have done the performance, we cannot always recollect what happened as clearly as we would like—whether things went well or not. As aware as we are and as concentrated as we should be, we dance for the moment. When the moment is gone, we are left with a largely intangible image. There are so many feelings going on during the performance: the anxiety and fears, the effort to remember what we've rehearsed, and the concentrated effort needed to make our bodies function as well as possible. But there is also an inspiration that is a great part of any performance—the little bit of something special, something that makes each person different from the other."

It can therefore be difficult to examine each performance, since questions that arise afterward are often asked in wonderment. Suppose a *pirouette* had ended awkwardly, off balance or aborted before the musical accent. A question afterward might be "What happened?" or "How did that happen?" Then one or the other of the partners makes assumptions or suggestions based on rather obvious information such as "Maybe you fell because you were leaning to the right." The other might respond with "If I had been centered in the beginning, I would not have compensated by leaning right, which threw me on the turn." This kind of repartee is an analytical way of discovering how not to make the same mistake again. It is not meant to be defensive and can be a means of finding solutions to the problems one does not wish to repeat. In a good partnership, it is an additional facet of the ongoing communication that makes the partnership work. Ballet mistresses and ballet masters sit in the audience watching the performance to follow through from the rehearsal process. They are a great help in clarifying details that, due to the state of tension dancers get into, they find difficult to analyze in a rational way.

There are no generalizations to be made about who takes the blame or who feels the worst when a performance has been less than perfect. Chivalry is alive and thriving in certain male dancers. In others, their male egos couldn't possibly allow them to take the blame even when they were wrong. Likewise, there are perfectionist females who are too insecure to deal well with mistakes that point out their all-too-human frailty and so cannot bear up under constructive criticism.

Cynthia: "It is quite amazing how one small incident can spoil a whole performance. For example, I had a performance of the full-length *Don Quixote* that was fairly smooth and yet, in the *pas de deux* the very last turn was not as good as it was in rehearsal. I was so disappointed, believing that I had let down both my partner and myself and ruined what, until then, I perceived to be a nearly flawless performance. Depending on a given mood, a large mistake can be laughed at in the knowledge that it was 'just one of those days'—or the smallest imperfection can be seen to be the biggest faux pas since the sinking of the *Titanic*. In the heat of the moment, it is easy to blow an entire event out of proportion and to take it so seriously that it becomes impossible to learn from the experience.

"Sometimes, when the *pas de deux* is seamless, I am gratified beyond belief. No solo has ever provided me with the satisfaction I have derived from a well-danced, sensitively portrayed *pas de deux*. Poetically speaking, when it comes to communicating life's great range of emotions, a *pas de deux* can ultimately be the finest balletic merging there is. And finally, the *pas de deux* is one of the most pleasurable experiences of the dance."

At some times more than others, dancers performing a *pas de deux* must concern themselves with the mechanics of the interaction between them. "An experience I once had on stage says much about the thinking sometimes necessary in making a dance work."

## "And There I Was. . . ." —Cynthia Harvey

I was both amused and nervous. There on stage during the intermission was Ross Stretton partnering an unlikely Giselle— Robert LaFosse! Only a few minutes earlier I had learned that I was to replace an ailing ballerina in the ballet *Giselle*. Ross was dancing the role of Albrecht, the male lead, and Robert, my only previous partner in this ballet, happened to be in the theatre. So

FIGURE 7-3   Cynthia Harvey and Robert LaFosse in American Ballet Theatre's
*Giselle*.

there were the two men, dancing the *pas de deux*. Robert was
brilliantly, if comically, portraying Giselle, the ethereal creature
in Act II of the ballet. From where I was warming up on stage,
I could overhear Robert saying, "Now, Cynthia likes it this way
here, and that way there," and, "she'll need a little help in this
section." "Don't forget to help her on the left side when she
rises onto *pointe* in *arabesque*," and, "She does this particular
timing on the little lift sequence before her *entrechat* solo." My
mind was racing back and forth between the amusing situation
I was witnessing and the one in which I would soon find myself—that of dancing with a new partner with virtually no rehearsal. I could not imagine that we could find the coordination

necessary to avert catastrophe, and I could hear myself saying, "This isn't going to work; no way is this going to work!"

I had been in the audience watching the performance in which Gelsey Kirkland was dancing Giselle and Carla Stallings was performing Myrtha, the Queen of the Wilis, for the first time. Arriving backstage during the first intermission to wish Carla good luck, I came upon a huddle of people outside Gelsey's dressing room. Suddenly all eyes were on me as if to say, "Cynthia, you're on!" Gelsey's infected blister would prevent her from continuing. My mind froze while my voice was saying, "I can't possibly—I haven't warmed up—I've never danced this role with Ross—I haven't rehearsed it—I don't have makeup on—Oh! I don't even have my shoes here!" (Not having shoes ready is quite unprofessional, but in this theatre—the Mann Music Center in Philadelphia—dressing room space had to be shared. We left our belongings in the hotel when we were not dancing.)

No excuse would get me out of this situation, so I agreed to dance Giselle. There was a flurry of activity—friends sewing shoes, others finding makeup and costume, while *I* was feeling I might be courting disaster! When I was finally "put together" physically, I still had to prepare mentally. I felt some relief when I reached the stage for a brief warm-up and saw Robert LaFosse trying to prepare Ross for the *pas de deux*.

Why were we so concerned about the *pas de deux*, which was only a part of the dancing we had to do? As a dancer, you strive for control of what you are doing—control of your body and mind. When dancing alone, you are in control. You know the choreography, you have learned your own technical capabilities and limitations, and you have to be concerned only about the subtleties of the conductor's interpretation of the music, the all-important floor, and the expectations of the audience. (The activity of dance itself is so challenging that although one cannot focus on the response of the audience while performing, an audience's expectation of a good performance matters a great deal.)

But the *pas de deux* is unique. Working with a partner means giving up some of that desired control. One must be prepared to share responsibility for interpreting the music and the choreography. Since there is physical contact between two people, there is no way the interaction can be ignored. This sensitivity to another person is what makes *pas de deux* the most exciting

*The Image and Experience of the*
Pas de Deux

*103*

form of dance for performers and audience alike. The audience—will *they* know that Ross and I have never danced this *pas de deux* together? That they will be vicariously sharing with us the experience of doing this dance for the first time?

Why was I so nervous about dancing with a new partner? Because we had not rehearsed together, and rehearsal builds confidence so that you know what is going to happen. You have to know your partner is going to be there for that catch when you are facing the other way and can't see him. He must know that his lift and his partner's jump will be synchronized in order to create the desired effect. The unpredictability that goes with working with a new partner instills a tension that can be quite disconcerting.

Dancers are always nervous when the unexpected is happening. As I was warming up, I was hearing not only Robert's comments to Ross, but also a great deal of laughter. Was that a dancer's mechanism for relieving tension? Perhaps. But all who observed this unfolding drama recognized the ridiculous sight of the two men dancing the beautiful *Giselle pas de deux*!

It was time for Act II to begin. The announcement "Cynthia Harvey will replace Gelsey Kirkland" was met with some surprise, as quite a few people had seen me in the audience during the first act. Suddenly the laughter and worry had to be submerged; Giselle was a *character* to be portrayed, an ethereal being that required a particular approach and bearing.

We began to dance the *pas de deux*, and I was very aware of my fear and nervousness. But Ross was incredibly cooperative, putting his own ego aside and doing what had to be done to present Giselle the way she had to be presented. I think sensitivity is the most important attribute of a partner. Ross demonstrated sensitivity magnificently that evening. Both of us had danced the ballet and knew the choreography and the characterization, but we had to concentrate very hard on the interaction taking place in the *pas de deux*. We couldn't just relax and let the dance happen. Rather than thinking about the ethereal floating image that Giselle is supposed to evoke, I was thinking, "I'm taller than Gelsey. Is he going to put me down from those lifts too soon? How am I going to adjust to the music if I hit the floor too soon?" Ross later said that he allowed me the freedom so that I could determine the timing and interpretation; he adjusted and followed.

At the end of the *pas de deux* we realized, "Well, we did it!" Everything worked. Was it luck? Yes, there is always some luck. Was it experience? Of course—both of us had worked with different partners for years and had developed a feel for where problems might lie and how to adjust. Was it hard work? Seldom do other aspects of dance require the intense concentration that partnering does. And the effort is greatest when there is the uncertainty of the first-time experience combined with the pressure of performing for an audience. But when a *pas de deux* works, it is one of the most thrilling experiences a dancer can have!

## Note

1. Jack Anderson, *Ballet and Modern Dance: A Concise History* (Princeton, NJ: Princeton Book Co., 1986).

# 8

# *A Physical Analysis of Partnering*

Mechanical considerations are important to dancers whether they are dancing alone or with a partner. In solo work, the dancer has only one body with which to deal. The constraints are those familiar considerations of the limits of technical capability and aspects of the environment less controllable by the dancer—the tempo of the music determined by a conductor or instrumentalist, the vagaries of the stage or studio floor and the shoes in contact with that floor, the size of the space available, and the variables of weather, lights, and mental state. The solo dancer copes alone with a physical environment that is, if not always controllable, at least mostly predictable: the floor does not suddenly change its position, and gravity does not suddenly release its hold on us.

FIGURE 8-1    Twyla Tharp and Mikhail Baryshnikov in Tharp's
*Once More, Frank* for American Ballet Theatre.

## Interactions Between Partners

A dancer working with a partner is faced with the same constraints of technical capability, music tempo, and physical space, but now must consider the more or less unpredictable interaction with another person who also has the same individual concerns faced by the solo dancer. That is, now *each of the two interacting dancers* has to be concerned about the music, floor, and lights in addition to a second person who is not (thank goodness!) totally predictable. Much effort in rehearsal is invested in trying to learn to predict how a partner will move—how the partner will interpret the music, and how the physical interaction between the two people is to be accomplished.

What sorts of physical interactions are considered "partnering"? Of course, part of the interaction may be mere touching, with the associated symbolic effect of the physical contact. But in terms of physical effects on movement, one dancer may be pulling or pushing on the other so as to create an acceleration in some direction. One may be helping another maintain balance, through contact at the waist, hands, or elsewhere. One may be helping another initiate a turn by exerting the required torque. Then there are lifts; one may be lifting the other by the waist or by other parts of the body, with the lifted dancer in a variety of positions—vertical, arched, or inverted, high or low.

Carrying out those interactions smoothly requires not only experience with a partner but a great deal of mutual sensitivity and coordination. For instance, if a man lifting his partner waits for her to jump before he lifts, he is too late. But if the woman waits for him to lift before she jumps, he will initially be lifting dead weight. In either case, the smoothness of the movement is lost. The two partners must be coordinated, and the means of achieving that coordination is what requires that dancers have mutual sensitivity to each other and to the music.

In order to deal with the way interactions between partners affect movement, we need first to discuss more carefully what we mean by movement. People can move in two ways. The first involves moving one part of the body relative to another, such as turning the head or lifting an arm or a leg. These movements could be carried out even if one were floating in free space, isolated from any other external physical influence. The second type of movement is motion of the body as a whole—a displacement of the body from one place to another or a rotation of the

FIGURE 8-2   Benjamin Pierce exerts a force on Julie Kent that allows her to accelerate.

body as a whole. These latter types of movement can occur only if there is interaction with the world outside one's own body, a world that may include a partner in addition to the floor and other more predictable objects. One may wish to start moving in some direction, or jump up, or start turning, but those movements are possible only if forces are exerted on the body by something outside the body.

A solo dancer has only two sources of force from outside his or her own body: gravity and the floor. Dancers working with partners can expand the range of their movement vocabulary because they are adding another source of interaction with the outside world—the interaction with a partner. Note that in traditional partnering, the roles of the two participants are not symmetric. The woman is performing normal dance movements, and it is *her* range of movement that is enhanced by the support of her partner. Aesthetically, the result is greater than the sum of the individual contributions, but it is the coordination of the two, and the help that the man can provide the woman, that creates that image. When dancing alone, the woman is responsible for everything that happens; when working with a partner, she shares that responsibility and the control that is needed to

*A Physical Analysis of Partnering*

meet that responsibility. In more contemporary choreography, it is more likely that both partners are contributing to each others' range of dance movement.

What is the basis of the physical interactions between two partners as they dance a *pas de deux*? When a dancer alone initiates a *pirouette* by exerting forces against the floor, the timing and magnitude of the forces that start the rotational motion are under the control of one body and one mind. That mind determines the timing and the strength needed, and stimulates the muscles to exert the necessary forces against the floor to start the turn. The experience of performing thousands of *pirouettes* during many years of training and performance is applied in this one finely tuned movement.

When a supported *pirouette* is performed—perhaps a supported *fouetté pirouette*, or "whip" turn, for which the forces initiating the turn are exerted by the partner—two minds must coordinate the movement together. (In the supported *fouetté*

FIGURE 8-3  Julie performing supported *pirouette* with Benjamin.

*pirouette*, the woman, standing on one straight supporting leg, moves the other straight leg from front to side as the partner exerts appropriate forces at her waist, thus allowing her to gain significant rotational motion by the time she moves into the *pirouette* position with one foot at the knee of the supporting leg.) Although the man standing behind the woman has some visual cues for her timing, the partners usually depend on a common interpretation of the music in order to coordinate their timing. And years of experience performing this movement with a variety of partners do not necessarily prepare dancers for the empathy needed to achieve the necessary coordination, an empathy that requires experience with a particular partner. Clearly, the timing and unity of interpretation cannot be perfect between two different human minds, but the audience is offered the opportunity of seeing how close the two minds can come to a perfect union. That is part of the magic of the *pas de deux*.

Dancers' movements result from forces acting upon them. A horizontal force will change the state of a dancer's linear movement across the floor; a vertical force may produce a lift; "push-pull" forces may produce rotations. Partners can be responsible for any of these agents of change in motion. A horizontal force exerted on a dancer may accelerate or slow her speed. If such forces are exerted at the center of gravity of her body, there is *only* a linear acceleration or deceleration, and no rotational motion. But a push from behind on the shoulders of a person standing at rest, above the center of gravity, will cause that person not only to accelerate, but also to topple forward. A push at the hips or waist, close to the center of gravity, will cause a smooth linear acceleration without toppling.

The toppling just described is one example of a rotational motion—in this case a rotation around a horizontal axis through the foot/floor contact point. But the most common rotational motion is that around a vertical axis, including all kinds of *pirouettes*.

## The Rotating Body

Suppose a dancer wishes to start his partner turning from a static position. The forces he must exert on her comprise the same sort of torque described in the chapter on *pirouettes*. In this case, the forces that act at different points of a body, producing a twisting movement or rotation, are exerted by a partner's

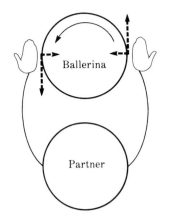

FIGURE 8-4 Hand positions for a supported *pirouette* in which the partner is providing the torque for the turn.

hands on the two sides of the ballerina's body. For instance, a partner may produce a *pirouette*-type rotation by pulling back on one side of a dancer's waist with one hand while pushing forward on the opposite side of the body with the other hand, as shown in figure 8-4 for a turn to the left.

Opening a door is an example of rotational motion. Although it involves an inanimate object, it is a familiar action the analysis of which applies to some dance movements. First, we all know it is not effective to attempt to open a door by pushing on it close to the hinge. A force at the axis of rotation exerts no torque. A force exerted a small distance from the hinge will succeed in opening the door, but only with difficulty. The rotational acceleration is small because the distance of the force from the axis is small. Pushing on the door near the edge farthest from the hinge is easiest.

It is a small stretch of the imagination to extend the ideas involved in the opening door to the case of a dancer turned by a partner. It is common, for instance, when two partners are in contact by means of their hands, for one to start turning because of a sideways force from the hand of the other. An example is a woman in *arabesque* facing her partner, starting to turn as a result of a force from her hand against her partner's hand. Accomplishing that move without losing balance is not easy; it is one of the movements analyzed in chapter 9.

As in linear motion, there is resistance to the change in the state of rotational motion. In this case this resistance, called "rotational inertia," depends not only on the mass but the way the mass is distributed relative to the rotation axis. The farther the mass is from the axis, the greater is the rotational inertia, and the smaller the resulting change in rotational motion that results from a torque. For example, if a dancer's arms are extended to the side, the rate of turn induced by a partner exerting a torque at the waist is less than if the arms are close to the body (closer to the vertical rotation axis). And a partner finds it more difficult to stop a dancer if her leg is extended while turning (as in *arabesque* or *à la seconde*) than if she is in a normal *pirouette* position with one foot at the knee of the supporting leg. Of course, part of *that* difficulty is due to the fact that the extended leg is usually in the way of the dancer who is trying to stop his partner.

# Balance

Early in a typical *pas de deux*, one often sees slow gestures and poses, frequently requiring careful balance, that gradually lead to more active movements later in the dance. These poses establish the image the dance is supposed to convey. The subtle tilts of the heads, gestures with the arms, and looks in the eyes tell the audience something about what to expect in the way of inter- action between these two people. For example, the images may convey soft and tender feelings of romantic love or tense expec- tations of explosive activity.

In these cases, support from a partner can allow for a wider variety of static positions for these gestures and poses than is possible for a dancer alone. A static position of a solo dancer implies balance, which requires the dancer's center of gravity to lie on a vertical line through the area of support at the floor. But other positions, not necessarily obeying that requirement, are possible when forces from a partner can help produce the con- dition of equilibrium. An example is a lunge, in which the center of gravity of a woman may be displaced horizontally far from her feet, but the displaced weight is supported by a vertical force exerted by the partner at her waist, torso, or other area of her body. Sometimes an image of tension or impending movement can be created by a dancer in an off-balance position held by the partner.

FIGURE 8-5   Here Julie is held in a static position that would be off balance if she were alone.

*Balance* for a person alone, interacting with the floor under the influence of gravity, was discussed in chapter 2. In order to maintain balance, subtle movements are necessary that result in the appropriate horizontal forces being exerted against the floor that keep the center of gravity directly above the supporting foot. Now suppose that the dancer has a partner and does not have to carry out those subtle movements to maintain her own balance. The partner can exert the appropriate horizontal forces on her that she needs, often at her waist, sometimes through contact at the hand or other places on the body. Note that some of the most impressive moments in a *pas de deux* occur when a woman, having established balance with the help of her partner, is suddenly released from his support and balances on her own. (A familiar example occurs in the third act of *The Sleeping Beauty* during the famous "Rose Adagio.") Achieving that necessary balanced condition with a partner prior to the release is a difficult feat, requiring sensitive control from the partner and timing of the release by the woman.

Maintaining a ballerina's balance when she is working with a partner is a challenge. She is used to dancing alone and depending on her own movements to maintain her own balance. If she tries to do that when a partner is trying to control her balance also, it doesn't work. He cannot know where her body is if she is carrying out those subtle adjusting movements while his hands are trying to be in the right place to support her. Teamwork is required in this most fundamental of interactions.

Consider now a case in which the woman must move while maintaining balance. Suppose she is holding an *arabesque* position facing stage left, standing on her left supporting leg with her right leg extended behind her. Her partner's hands are at her waist. Now she moves into a *penchée*, pivoting forward on her supporting leg, her upper body bending forward, and the working leg rising toward the vertical. If she is *en pointe*, it is her partner's job to maintain her balance while she carries out this movement. Since her center of gravity shifts due to the forward and backward movement of her upper body and working leg, her partner must shift the location of her waist appropriately in order to maintain her balance. Actually, women who have less of an arch in the supporting foot usually find it easier to stay *en pointe* if they are held in a position slightly forward of a true balance, because the forward weight of the body helps to keep the toes under the supporting foot, as demonstrated in figure 8–7. A woman with well-arched feet may prefer to be very close to true balance. A good partner will be sensitive to such subtle differences in the dancers with whom they work. And there is more to the partner's job in this simple movement than has just been described. He provides some lift at her waist, and some

FIGURE 8–7 Julie is supported slightly in front of a balanced position in this *arabesque penchée*.

torque and lift to help her rise to recover from the *penchée* position.

A partner's two hands at the woman's waist provide the strongest support for her movements. But sometimes contact is more tenuous. An example of a balance with contact only at the hands occurs in the "Rose Adagio" of *The Sleeping Beauty*. In this section Aurora, the title character, dances with a group of four suitors vying for her hand in marriage. She dances with each of them in turn, and one of the more challenging sections involves long balances of Aurora in *attitude* (similar to *arabesque* but with a bent back leg), supported by one hand by each of the suitors in turn, balancing alone in the transitions between partners. (This position is seen in figures 8-6 and 8-8.) She faces stage right, facing each suitor in *attitude* on her right supporting leg with her left leg behind her, her right hand in contact with his right hand. The sequence is later repeated, this time with a full promenade in a circle with each partner in turn. The dancer must remain facing her partner while balanced *en pointe* throughout each of these long maneuvers, a most impressive feat!

If Aurora is balanced with contact at the hand of a partner, everything is fine. But as before, she is likely to find herself eventually slightly off balance, particularly during the promenades in the second sequence. How does she adjust for this loss of balance? If she pushes sideways against her partner's hand, she can indeed regain balance because of the horizontal force that his hand exerts on her in response. But such a horizontal force exerted on her body some distance from the vertical axis of potential rotation around her supporting foot will result in an uncontrolled rotation of her body away from her orientation facing him. That is, suppose she starts falling toward her left. If she pushes toward the left against his hand, the response of his hand is to push toward her right, which not only moves her center of gravity back toward her right, helping her to regain balance, but also starts a rotation of her body to the right, away from its orientation facing him.

How, then, does she maintain her balance? She must exert against his hand not a linear force, but a *twisting torque*. That is, in the case described above, her hand must exert a clockwise twist against his hand to create the response that corrects balance without resulting in the unwanted rotation. (A detailed description of this situation has been previously published.[1])

## Accelerating Motions with a Partner

Another way a partner can make movements possible that would be impossible for a solo dancer is by accelerating a dancer linearly. A solo dancer can accelerate only by exerting an appropriate force against the floor, which means that the movement must start with some toppling motion so that the feet don't run out from under the rest of the body. But with a partner, accelerations can take place from balanced positions, or even from positions that lean off balance in the direction opposite to the direction of acceleration. For example, consider a dancer in *arabesque* position on her right supporting leg facing stage right, with her left leg and hand behind her, and a partner behind her as well. She leans forward (toward stage right), but her partner pulls back on her left hand and accelerates her toward stage left. As she starts moving in that direction, she may execute a *fouetté* that rotates her to face the direction in which she starts moving. The effect is that of a tension pulling her in a direction opposite to that toward which her body is trying to move, and is an effect difficult to accomplish without a partner as a source of force, both physical and psychological.

*A Physical Analysis of Partnering*

Similarly, static positions that would be off balance for a solo dancer can be maintained by the forces provided by a partner. With less force from the partner, the leaning *arabesque* described above can be a static pose with a powerful effect of unresolved tension.

Suppose a dancer wishes to move in a circular path. If alone, a dancer has only the floor as a source of force directed toward the inside of the circle—a force necessary for such a curved path. The dancer must be leaning toward the inside of the circle in order to be able to exert that force between the feet and the floor, for the same reason that a road is banked in turns. But if a partner is present, that person can provide the force directed toward the center of the circular path that allows for that motion. For instance, both partners can be rotating around each other, as is often observed in "pivot turns" in ballroom dance or in some folk dance movements. Both partners

FIGURE 8-9   Benjamin holding Julie in a "fish" position sometimes seen at the end of a *pas de deux*.

FIGURE 8-10   Julie and Benjamin show the "swan" position.

can be in off-balance positions such that, without the other person, they would fly off, away from the circular path. Again the image is that of a body being held in a path or pose from which it would like to break away.

A common way of concluding a *pas de deux* is for the man to be supporting his partner in some climactic pose at the end of the musical phrase or section. These poses may involve lifts, discussed in chapter 10, or other supported poses, such as a "fish" or "swan" position. In both of these, the woman is held off the floor by her partner, in an arched front-side-down position facing the audience. In the "fish," shown in figure 8-9, the partner supports her weight with one hand on her thigh and the other under her ribs near her hips. In the "swan," shown in figures 8-10 and 8-11, the woman's weight is supported on her partner's forward (bent) leg, while she prevents her upper body from falling forward and down by clamping one of her legs

*A Physical Analysis of Partnering*

119

FIGURE 8-11  The authors and Benjamin working on the "swan" pose.

behind his back. The demand on the woman's back muscles is great, and the position is not easy to achieve.

Other final poses may involve a lunge, or fall, in which the woman falls to an inclined position, supported by her partner's arm around her rib cage. Although this position looks straightforward, there are potential pitfalls not obvious to an observer. If the woman tries to keep her upper body more vertical by bending at the waist, then the part of her body that her partner is trying to support with his arm is closer to vertical, and a vertical supporting force becomes very difficult. On the other hand, if his arm is too high on her body, he may be forcing her into that bent position. Experience and training allows partners to find the most comfortable way of achieving this sort of position and producing the desired line.

## To the Next Step

Constant movement is seldom seen in dance, any more than entirely static positions are viewed. Both are necessary to create the aesthetic images desired. Static poses, when used as breathing moments in a dance that is mostly movement, help expand the range of images possible. There are subtleties in the ways dancers use forces between themselves and their environment in order to maintain these balanced positions for just the right length of time, sometimes using large forces between partners, sometimes only a light touch.

Dancers moving alone have the entire range of human movement available to them within the constraints of their technical capability and the constraints imposed by the physical reality of the floor and gravity as the sole sources of external force. Dancers working with partners must deal with the uncertainties arising because of the lack of total individual control, but they have the advantage of the increased range of movements made possible by interactions with another body and mind. Those interactions expand the range of possible motion through the medium of the forces between the two bodies. How are those forces exerted? What movements are made possible by the addition of a partner as a part of a dancer's environment?

Two categories of partnered dance movement have been mentioned—turns and lifts. Turns of many kinds are discussed in chapter 9, and lifts, a most impressive aspect of partnering, in chapter 10.

## Note

1. K. Laws, "Precarious Aurora—an Example of Physics in Partnering," *Kinesiology for Dance* 12 (August 1980): 2-3.

# 9

# *The Mechanics of Partnered Turns*

Turning dancers are an integral part of virtually every dance ever choreographed. These rotations can involve *pirouettes*—turns around a vertical axis on one supporting leg; *promenades*—slow, controlled turns around a vertical axis; and even impressive turns in the air. Many of these turns can be done by dancers alone; others require the interaction of partners. *Pirouettes* performed alone were analyzed in chapter 4. We will now turn our attention to the mechanics and techniques of partnered turns, which are found in virtually every choreographed dance for partners.

A normal supported *pirouette* consists of a woman executing a turn with the help of a partner behind her, usually with his

FIGURE 9-1   Cynthia Harvey and Guillaume Graffin turning in a scene from Kenneth MacMillan's *Manon* for American Ballet Theatre.

hands on her waist. The partner can help maintain her balance during the turn, and can help provide the torque to initiate the turn or the reverse torque to stop the turn in the desired orientation. First let us examine the process of balancing during the turn.

## Balance During a Supported *Pirouette*

A dancer performing a smooth and pleasing supported *pirouette* should be as close to balanced as possible, particularly at the end of the turn. Why is it difficult to maintain balance in a supported *pirouette*? First, it is unlikely that any *pirouette* can be started with the center of gravity so precisely positioned that it is directly over the point of the supporting foot. Second, because a partner is there to help control balance, a supported *pirouette* often lasts longer than a *pirouette* performed alone, which allows more time for toppling off balance. It is also true that the body performing a *pirouette* is not in a symmetric configuration, so there is always some inherent wobble of body mass around the axis of rotation. This wobble can be exaggerated if the woman is also trying to keep from hitting her partner with her knee during the rotation. Finally, the turning dancer's partner cannot hold any part of her body, since she is rotating; she is constantly slipping through his hands.

First let us suppose the ballerina is in a nonrotating *pirouette* position (supporting leg straight, *en pointe*, with the gesture leg raised to the side with its foot at the knee of the supporting leg). It is clear that if her center of gravity is displaced horizontally from that region directly above the small area of support at the floor, the partner merely has to exert a force at her waist in the appropriate direction to return her to a balanced position. If meanwhile she is trying to regain her own balance by the techniques described in chapter 2, she is making her partner's job difficult. And the partner's contribution to her balance *is* necessary if she is to maintain balance longer than she would dancing alone. But one of the hardest jobs for a woman learning to be partnered is to prevent herself from doing those balance-regaining body manipulations that are so important when she is dancing solo. She is far more often dancing alone than with a partner, so those subtle adjusting movements become habit. But those same movements prevent a partner from knowing where her body is and what he has to do to correct for her imbalance.

Now suppose that she is rotating. Her job is to be as close to balance as possible at the beginning of the turn, but to avoid trying to maintain her balance once she is turning. It is more difficult, however, for her partner to control her balance when she is rotating than when she is not. If her waist were frictionless, then forces between his hands and her waist could easily be directed such as to return her to balance. But there is a friction force also, in a direction tangent to the hand/waist contact. When she is balanced, that friction force will be the same from both hands. But if he is exerting a greater force with one hand than the other in order to move her back toward balance from a sideways displacement, the friction force from that hand will be greater also, and she will have a tendency to move forward or backward.

That is, suppose the woman is starting to topple to the right, while turning to her right. Her partner uses his right hand to push her back toward the left. But if he exerts more force against her waist with his right hand than with his left, then the greater resulting friction force will cause her to be pushed forward as well as to the left. If she is turning to the *left* and is falling toward the right, then her partner's attempt to bring her back to the left will thrust her backward. An experienced partner will automatically accommodate to that tendency, and will exert a force with his right hand toward the left *and back or front*. The first of these situations is diagrammed in figure 9–2.

An experienced ballerina will usually perform the *pirouettes* close to a balanced position so that only subtle forces are needed from the partner. An experienced partner will be sensitive to subtle imbalances so that he can adjust the hand positions and forces quickly enough to prevent disaster. In fact, if the ballerina is slightly off balance to the rear, the best appearance is attained, because her partner's hands can remain slightly in back of her, shifting positions as necessary without moving in front of her in clear view of the audience. He never has to have a hand in front to pull her back, a movement that can compromise the aesthetic appearance of the *pirouette*.

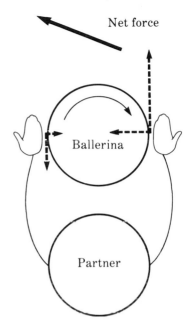

a. Unbalanced toward right

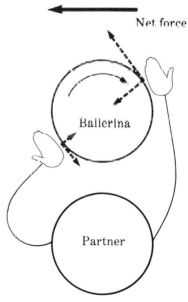

b. Unbalanced toward right, corrected.

FIGURE 9–2a,b  Hand positions for off-balance supported *pirouettes*, viewed from above. a. Unbalanced to the right. b. Unbalanced to the right, corrected.

FIGURE 9-3 This pirouette has been stopped, with the aid of the partner, when the body is in a position facing away from the audience, as in the end of the first section of the "Black Swan" *pas de deux* from *Swan Lake*.

## Control of Rotation in Supported *Pirouettes*

We have seen that a solo dancer has only the *floor* to use as a source of forces that will produce either linear or rotational motion. In many cases, the floor is used for the horizontal forces required to initiate a turn, and the dancer needs no help from the partner for the turning action itself. But a partner *can* exert forces on her waist in a direction such as to contribute to the rotation she is otherwise beginning herself, or to supply the entire torque that produces the rotation. Note, however, that the forces and torques required to control the turn must be carried out at the same time as those required for maintaining balance as discussed above. The partner might also be called upon to exert the forces necessary to stop her turn at the appropriate time and in the appropriate orientation. While she usually finishes facing the audience, sometimes—for example, in the "Black Swan" *pas de deux*—the turn ends with the dancer's back to the audience, but with the upper back and head arched back so that her face is toward the audience, as demonstrated by Julie and Benjamin in figure 9-3.

FIGURE 9-4 This is a sequence of views showing the beginning of a supported *fouetté* turn. The torque for this turn comes totally from the forces exerted by the supporting partner. The final rotational momentum produced by that torque is enhanced because Julie stores the momentum in her leg while Benjamin is still exerting forces at her waist.

Let us examine *pirouettes* that are performed with the woman starting *en pointe* and depending totally on her partner for the torque that gives her the rotational momentum for the turn. That sounds simple; he just pulls back with one hand and pushes forward with the other when it is time to start the turn. The problem is that she quickly starts rotating as soon as those forces are exerted, and he is no longer able to continue exerting the necessary forces. The resulting turn rate is not very rapid.

But recall the *fouetté* turns described in chapter 4. That sequence involved a transfer of rotational momentum back and forth between the rotating leg and the body as a whole. A similar mechanism can be used in starting a partnered *pirouette*, allowing the partner to extend the length of time he can exert a torque. This technique involves the woman storing the rotational momentum that her partner generates with his hands in a part of her body that can rotate while her waist remains stationary so that his hands can continue to exert the required forces. She uses an extended free leg moving from front to side for that purpose. So, as shown in the sequence in figure 9–4, the movement starts with the woman *en pointe* on her left supporting leg, with her right leg extended a little to the left of front, and her partner's hands at her waist. He starts pulling back with his right hand and pushing forward with his left, while she causes her right leg to revolve from front to her right side. During that time her torso, head, and supporting leg do not rotate, so her partner continues to exert those forces with his hands. Then,

after she has gained a significant rotational momentum, she brings her leg in to a normal *pirouette* position with the foot at the knee of the supporting left leg. The rotational momentum stored in that moving right leg is quickly transferred to the body as a whole, and a rapid rotation results!

When performing that supported *fouetté* turn, as it is called, seldom do the participants or the observers realize what a marvelous, coordinated mechanism is at work in order to extend the length of time the woman's partner can exert a torque on her and achieve a greater turn rate. It becomes clear why certain aspects of that movement are important if it is to be carried out effectively. For instance, if her rotating leg takes a shortcut into the knee rather than moving all the way to the side, her whole body starts absorbing the rotational momentum significantly sooner, and the resulting total rotational momentum cannot be as great. Similarly, if her partner is not prepared to exert the forces when she starts the leg rotating, the rest of her body will react by rotating in the opposite direction, since there are no forces from her partner to keep her torso facing the original direction.

There is another form of supported *pirouette*, called a "finger turn." The dancer again begins *en pointe,* with the right leg extended to the front and a little to the left. She pushes with her left hand backward against his extended left hand in order to initiate the turn, again swinging her right leg from front to side to extend the length of time she is able to push off from his hand. The right leg then returns to the normal *pirouette* position. Balance is maintained by her right hand clasped loosely around a vertical finger of his right hand held above her head as a pivot. The mechanical principles involved in this turn are similar to those applied to the supported *fouetté* turn shown in figure 9–4.

Several aspects of this turn are important. First, the partner must be sufficiently tall to hold his finger strongly above the woman's head while she is *en pointe*. In these days of tall female dancers, that requirement is not as easily met as one might think! Second, it is crucially important for the woman to have her body well aligned along that vertical rotation axis, with the hand held *directly* above the supporting foot rather than somewhat to the front, which is a more natural location. Since the hand determines the rotation axis, a hand in front of the vertical line will cause her partner to have to move his hand in a circle while

her right leg, facing stage left toward her partner and maintaining balance by means of contact between her right hand and his, as shown in the first view in figure 9-7. Suppose that from this position she must start turning to her right, bringing the free left leg from *arabesque* around to her left side (to *à la seconde*), thence into *pirouette* position with its foot at the knee of the right leg. Since she is *en pointe*, the only source of force for her to begin her rotation is her partner's hand. Now if she pushes to her left against his hand, that will certainly produce a force acting along a line some distance from the axis of rotation, and the resulting torque will indeed produce a rotation to her right. But that sideways force also will be a net force that tends to cause her to topple off balance to the right.

How does she avoid the problem of toppling caused by the same force that allows her to rotate? One technique is to exert a *twisting torque* against her partner's hand so that, although there is no net force that would tend to make her lose balance, there is a twisting torque *at the hand* that acts to cause the body to rotate. That can be difficult to carry out because, since the hands are relatively small, the twisting forces required can be very large. Remaining close to balance so that the necessary

*The Mechanics of Partnered Turns*

131

forces are small enough to be manageable is one of the challenges to the dancers preforming this movement. This is exactly the situation described in chapter 8, applied to the "Rose Adagio" in *The Sleeping Beauty*.

The other technique, which seems to be unconsciously applied by dancers with partnering experience, is that she makes herself lean a bit to the left just before the start of the turn, so that with no force against her partner's hand, she would topple to the left. Then, when she does exert a force toward the left against his hand, his hand exerts the corresponding force to the right, which not only produces the torque to start her turning, but also brings her back toward the balanced condition. That is a subtle adjustment for the body to make subconsciously, but experiments have shown that such an adjustment is indeed carried out. (An experiment that demonstrates that effect is to remove the partner's hand just as the woman is about to exert a force to start the turn. In most cases she does topple off balance to her left.) What is remarkable here is that the woman must anticipate the movement in a timely way, and actually cause herself to be off balance in order to carry out the turn smoothly.

"Pencil turns" are another form of partnered *pirouette* from *arabesque*, this with the partner behind the ballerina, upstage of her. Suppose she is again facing stage left, with her left leg extended behind her. Now she brings her left leg down close to her supporting right leg while her partner exerts a torque on her waist. She gains rotational momentum and a rather large turning speed, since her legs being close together keep her rotational inertia small. After she has turned through several rotations, she stops again in the same *arabesque* position from which she started. Clearly the coordinated timing is important, both to start the turn in synchronism and to stop it with the dancer facing the desired direction.

*Promenades* are slow, controlled turns around a vertical axis on one supporting foot, often involving the partner walking around the woman so that their orientation with respect to each other remains constant. When the man walks in a circle while rotating his partner through one revolution, it is clear that he is exerting appropriate forces with his hand or hands on some part of her body to initiate the turning movement. He may have hands at her waist, or there may be hand-to-hand contact. In the latter case, the most common difficulty is maintaining her balance, which is difficult if the man moves away from or toward his partner (and her fixed axis of rotation) instead of walking in a circle. Adjustments must constantly be made in order to allow the woman to maintain an aesthetically pleasing line while maintaining balance during this promenade.

A *promenade* with contact between only one hand of each partner (with the woman in *attitude* position on one supporting pointed foot, for instance) looks simple, involving one dancer walking around the other while they remain facing each other. But it is difficult partly because of a problem similar to that described earlier for a *pirouette* initiated from the force from one hand of the partner. In this case the woman must maintain her balance while rotating, *and* maintain her orientation facing her partner, having only her partner's hand as a source of forces while that hand is some distance from the rotation axis. This situation was described in chapter 8 in a discussion of the "Rose Adagio" in *The Sleeping Beauty*.

Many types of turns are supported by a partner's hands at the waist. If the rotating body were symmetric, the waist would be centered on the rotation axis, and the hands could remain in one position during the rotation. But turns almost always occur on one supporting leg, so the symmetry is broken by the fact that one foot is on the floor and the other leg is lifted. The partner must be very aware of that changing position of the waist that occurs during a rotation. An example of such a turn is a quick 180° *fouetté* turn supported by a partner's hands at the waist.

Suppose a dancer is in *arabesque* on the left supporting leg, facing stage left, as shown in the first view of figure 9-8. She brings her right leg from *arabesque* position behind her through a position close to her supporting leg, and continues moving it to a position in front of her, while she remains facing stage left. When that right leg arrives at the front, she rotates her body to the left, leaving the right leg where it was, so that she ends the movement in arabesque facing stage right. At the beginning of the movement, her partner is holding her waist, keeping her in a balanced position. But because the mass of her leg is behind her, her waist is somewhat in front of her supporting foot. Now when her right leg moves down and through to her front, her partner must move her torso toward stage right (shifting his weight in order to do so) to prevent her from being off balance toward the left (her front) when her leg is in its new orientation.

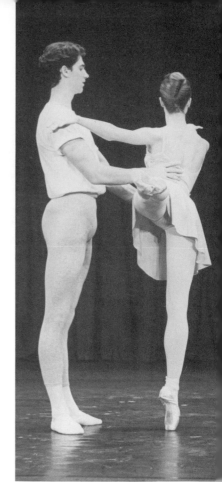

FIGURE 9-8   A *fouetté* 180° "flip" turn from *arabesque*, as seen from the side. (The audience is to the right in the photograph.) This is a challenging movement to partner because of the coordination of the torque necessary for her turn and the changes in location of her waist when she is balanced in the three positions shown during the sequence of the total movement.

Then, when the rotation begins for the half turn, he must provide the torque, and must also shift her torso toward him some distance, since the supporting leg, which was the leg closest to him, is now the leg farthest from him. These subtle shifts in how the partner's body must be held in order to maintain balance can be quite complicated and are learned only by much practice. Of course, a further complication is that every dancer's body is different, with different mass distribution and different ways of moving.

*The Mechanics of Partnered Turns*

## A Final Turn

Turns in dance are impressive movements. Partnered turns require a great deal of coordination, since the forces between partners are often quite large, and the control necessary to maintain the aesthetic image while rotating, sometimes rapidly, is very difficult. A viewer who understands that any turning motion requires a torque from somewhere can recognize that one challenge for dancers is to make a turn as smooth as possible by coordinating the use of necessary forces. Controlling both the balance and the rate of turn is another aspect that requires the cooperation of both partners. When that coordination is missing, one can see unexpected and often distracting results. When these movements do work, it is a result of a remarkable ability of the dancers to coordinate their efforts in order to enhance the image of dance they are projecting.

# 10

# *The Mechanics of Lifts*

One dancer lifting another is often seen in partnered dance. Clearly, a dancer jumping without the aid of a partner cannot achieve the height, the duration, or the positions possible when lifted by a partner. The intent of the lift may be to create an image of gentle floating for an ethereal creature such as Giselle, or an image of defying gravity by flying through the air, or simply an image of extending the range of motion beyond that possible for a single, unaided dancer. The lift may represent the stature implied by height, as for a queen or princess who has a lofty position relative to those around her. A lift to a partner's shoulder is common at the climax of a *pas de deux* in classical ballet.

The lifts described in this chapter, in which the woman is lifted by the man, are those familiar to observers of classical ballet, although the principles can be applied to any style of

FIGURE 10-1   Susan Jaffe and Alexander Godunov perform a lift in American Ballet Theatre's "Pas d'Esclave," a *pas de deux* from Petipa's *Le Corsaire*.

FIGURE 10-2 The highest point in a straight lift.

dance, for any combination of genders of partners. For simplicity, the examples will be those from the familiar ballet vocabulary. The movements dealt with here range from low lifts, in which the woman is never very high off the ground although her weight is borne by her partner, to high overhead lifts. They may range from "temporary" lifts, in which the woman is effectively performing a jump extended in time and height by the supporting force of the partner, to extended lifts, in which her weight is totally supported by the partner as she maintains a position aloft for a longer time.

The appearance of ease or difficulty in a lift may be deceptive. In Balanchine's *Theme and Variations*, for instance, there are a number of lifts, none very high, but all very difficult because they require the man to lift the woman with her weight in front of him and keep her supported there for an extended time. In the same choreographer's *Concerto Barocco*, the man carries his partner slowly across the stage for almost half a minute, alternating between an upright position in front of him and an inverted position over his back. These lifts are more difficult than they appear.

Proper technique is always important in dance, not only to allow dancers to create the desired aesthetic images, but also to help avoid injury. The physical dangers are particularly great when dancers are working with partners, which requires that they coordinate movements that may involve forces, heights, and speeds not attainable by solo dancers. These dangers are particularly notable in lifts. A common problem faced by male dancers is low back injury that often results from the lifting required in partnering. Women face the potential danger of falling from sizable heights in partnered lifts. In fact, the potential danger in some movements contributes to the appeal to an audience. There is a thrill both for dancers and for their audiences when a woman is held eight feet in the air with her back toward the floor, supported only by her partner's hands.

## The Straight Lift

Let us start with one of the simplest lifts—a straight lift in which the woman remains vertical while her partner lifts her by his hands at her waist, from a stance directly behind her. Even in this simple lift, there are several questions, potential problems, and technical dos and don'ts. There are considerations of the most effective relative sizes of the two dancers and the way they coordinate their respective motions. There is the proper technique for the woman, involving her preparation, jump, and position in the air. There is the proper technique for the man, involving the position of his hands, his stance behind the woman, and the muscles he uses to perform the lift.

It may appear that the smaller the woman, the easier it is for her partner to lift her. But note that if she is short, he must bend lower in a preparation position in order to place his hands where they must be to perform the lift. Lifting a person is more difficult when the lift must start closer to the floor. Not only is the back inclined at the hip, with a resulting strain on the lumbar spine, but it is more difficult to exert a force with the legs when the knees are bent more than 90°. One reason dance companies often select female dancers who are tall and slender is that partners find it easier to lift that type of body.

For proper technique in this lift, as in others, the lifter should delay straightening his legs until the arms are well on their way to being straight. The leg muscles are substantially stronger than the arm muscles and can be used for much of the lifting. As the arms or the legs approach full straight extension, the vertical force they can exert becomes larger. In the diagram shown in figure 10-3, the bent arm in the first case can exert only one-quarter as much lifting force as in the second case, for the same torque at the elbow and shoulder. Therefore the arms should be straightened as much as possible while most of the upward impetus is coming from the woman's jump. As the momentum from her jump is expended, his arms and legs take over for the later part of the lift. The lift then appears most smooth and flowing.

Of course, the woman must have strength also, as she must help in the lifting process by jumping. One might ask how much of the energy that goes into a lift is provided by the woman and how much by her partner. That question is easy to answer by observing how high she can jump by herself in a similar movement. If her center of gravity rises somewhat less than one foot when she jumps unassisted, that height is a measure of the work done against gravity in the jumping process, which is equal to the increase in mechanical energy in the jump. When a partner lifts her as she contributes the same magnitude of jumping force,

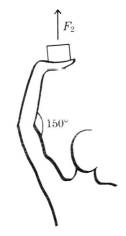

FIGURE 10-3   When the arms are almost straight, a greater vertical force may be exerted than when they are bent. In the case shown here, the magnitude of the force $F_2$ is about four times the magnitude of $F_1$ for the same muscle force and torque at the elbow and shoulder.

*The Mechanics of Lifts*

her center of gravity may rise three feet or more. Since the work done, and the corresponding mechanical energy contributed to the woman's mass, is proportional to the height, the man contributes perhaps 75 percent of the energy.

One characteristic of any lift that is very important in determining the difficulty for the lifting partner is the position of the woman's center of gravity relative to the location of her partner's hands on her body. If her center of gravity is located on a vertical line that passes directly between his hands, then a vertical force from his hands is all that is required to support her in the air. But if that center of gravity lies, for instance, in front of his hands when they are at her waist, then she would tend to rotate forward during the lift unless he can also exert a twisting torque to keep her oriented vertically. A common mistake made by a female dancer learning this straight lift technique is neglecting to keep her body straight. There is a tendency to lean forward at the waist while in the air, thus displacing the center of gravity forward and making it difficult for her partner to maintain her vertical position in the air. (See figure 10-4.) A fear of the height of the lift or a desire to keep her feet away from her partner's body may motivate that flaw in body position.

In order to make the lift as comfortable as possible for the woman, her partner must place his hands under her rib cage. Actually, since skin and clothing do slide over the body to some extent, the partner must start with his hands significantly below her rib cage. One reason the wide part of a classical tutu is below the waist is to allow the partner access to the location on her body that he must utilize for lifts and supported *pirouettes*. And women find it more comfortable if the heels of his hands are used more than a squeezing grip with his fingers. Finally, his stance must be sufficiently close to his partner that he is not lifting her weight too far in front of him, which would involve large torques in his shoulders and back. On the other hand, he must hold her far enough in front of him that he does not arch his lower back, a position that is conducive to lumbar spine injury.

Why are men who often perform lifts plagued with lower back problems? Part of the reason involves the timing of the vertical force exerted during the lift. Experiments have been carried out at Dickinson College (Pennsylvania) in which force sensors were used to measure the upward force exerted by the

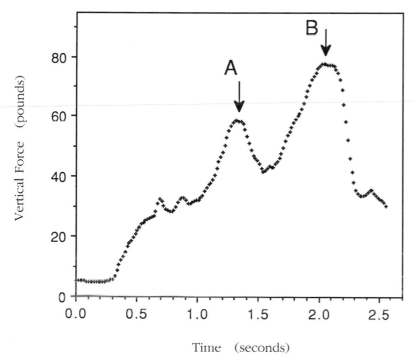

## Force vs. Time for Vertical Lift

FIGURE 10-5 This graph represents the way the vertical force exerted by the lifter on his partner during a straight lift varies with time. Point *A* is early in the lift during ascent, and Point *B* occurs just before the return of the lifted dancer's feet to the floor.

man's hands on his partner during the straight lift described here. (This lift involves an ascent and an immediate descent, with no time spent in a static position aloft.) Those measurements show that the force is large during the early part of the lift; smaller near the peak, when he is allowing her to start to accelerate back down for the descent; then *greatest* just before she arrives back at the floor. (See graph in figure 10-5.) Thus the greatest force he must exert occurs when his arms are low and his back is most inclined at the waist. At those times her center of gravity is farthest in front of him, requiring the greatest strain on his lower back. Why is the force greatest when she is closest to the ground, particularly on the descent? First, there is the need to propel her upward early in the lift in order to achieve the acceleration necessary to accomplish the movement quickly. Upon descent, he is motivated to prevent injury to his partner, and thus will try to cushion her descent as much as possible as she approaches the floor. Not only must he cushion the descent *without* the help that she can provide when jumping upward at the beginning of the movement, but his muscles can exert greater force when she is descending than when she is rising, because of an interesting characteristic of muscle activity. Muscles can exert a large force when they are undergoing *eccentric* contraction, in which the working muscles stretch and the movement (in this case, downward) is in a direction opposite to the force he is exerting. Less force is possible during *concentric* contraction, in which the muscles contract and cause movement in the same direction as the exerted force. So the force the man is able to exert to support his partner is greater on the descent than the initial ascent.

What should lifters do to alleviate the strain on the back during lifts? First, the back should be inclined as little as possible by bending the legs instead. The legs must work harder, but some of the strongest muscles in the body are the leg muscles used in the lifting process. It is sometimes observed that the man will allow the woman to slide down the front of his body on descent, thereby minimizing the distance her center of gravity is in front of him, and allowing him to *bend his legs* on descent rather than inclining his back. Although this technique is not as pleasing aesthetically, it may be preferable to an otherwise too rapid descent.

An impressive version of this straight lift is performed with the woman undergoing a full turn around a vertical rotation axis at the peak of the lift. In order to accomplish that more difficult feat, the upward lifting force must be sufficiently large that the woman coasts upward in free flight long enough for her partner to exert a torque at her waist and let her rotate freely between his hands. Clearly, he can exert no upward force on her while she is turning, as his hands cannot move around the circular path along with her waist. When she has completed the full turn, his hands again clamp on her waist, stopping the turn and beginning to cushion her descent. Thus there must be enough vertical motion to perform a "throw and catch" rather than just a lift.

FIGURE 10-6   a. An *arabesque* lift with the appropriate forces exerted by the lifter. b. An *arabesque* lift in which the lifter fails to apply the torque necessary, allowing the dancer to rotate out of the *arabesque* position.

## Other Front Lifts

Another common lift is an *arabesque* lift, in which the woman holds an *arabesque* position with one leg extended behind her and the other vertically beneath her while she is lifted or carried by her partner. If he is supporting her by her waist, there is a problem that can often be observed. Note that a significant part of the woman's mass is behind her when her leg is extended in *arabesque*, as shown in figure 10-6a. In fact, if she has a good arch in her back, her upper body and lower leg can be close to vertical while the other leg is extended to the back, allowing much less of her body mass to be in front of the support from her partner's hands at her waist than in back of that support. If he exerts only an upward force at her waist, she will swing like a pendulum so that her back leg droops, her lower leg moves forward, and her upper body leans back, as seen in figure 10-6b.

FIGURE 10-7  A *grand jeté* carry, showing the gradual rotation of the dancer's orientation through the trajectory.

That problem is prevented if the man exerts a torque on her body in addition to the supporting force—a torque that attempts to rotate her upper body forward, as Benjamin is doing in figure 10-6a. He accomplishes that torque by moving his upper hand higher on her back and pushing forward, while supporting most of her weight with his lower hand.

Sometimes the desired effect for a lift is for the woman's body to appear to travel an arching path during a traveling *grand jeté* lift, so that she starts facing upward somewhat, then rotates to an orientation facing a little downward at the end of the movement. To accomplish that, her partner must exert an even larger torque to cause her to rotate in a direction opposite to the natural tendency during the duration of the lift.

In another form of *arabesque* lift, the woman faces the audience, again on her left supporting leg with her right leg extended to the back. Her partner, also facing the audience, places his right shoulder under her right thigh. His hands support her under her rib cage directly in front, and her left leg is vertical directly in front of his body. This lift is made difficult by the fact that he must start from a very low position in a deep *plié*, then straighten up with her on his shoulder. Since she starts in *arabesque* position on one supporting leg, she can provide little jump to help at the beginning. And he must bear a sizable part of her weight on his hands extended well in front of his body, not the easiest position from which to exert an upward force.

*The Mechanics of Lifts*

FIGURE 10-8 An *arabesque* "press" lift.

## Overhead Lifts

Overhead lifts are impressive in that the height achieved by the woman is great, creating an expansive and grand image to the audience. There is a resulting difficulty for both partners, along with a greater danger than for smaller lifts.

A lift in which the woman is again in the *arabesque* position is the so-called "press lift," shown in figure 10-8. In this case the man lifts her to a position over his head, supporting her with one hand on her waist and the other on the thigh of the extended leg. Benjamin is lifting Julie with his right hand below her right rib cage, again nearly at her hip, and his left hand on the thigh of her left (extended) leg. This lift can be a stable lift in which her center of gravity is directly above his shoulders and feet, with his arms straight and therefore able to exert an upward force with relative ease. There are two problems for him. One is that he receives very little help from his partner, since she starts in a balanced position on one leg, often *en pointe*, not a position conducive to an effective jump. The other is that he must have sufficient flexibility in his shoulders and elbows to allow his arms to be straight overhead while his back is straight and not arched. An arch in the lower back while supporting weight overhead is an invitation to injury!

There are other forms of overhead lifts. In one particularly impressive example, the woman, traveling or stationary in front of the man, jumps up and arches backward at the same time, while her partner, initially facing her back, lifts her with his hands on her lower back. She arrives inverted over his head, as shown in the photograph in figure 10-9. In this lift, she must arch quickly enough in the process to assure that she is

FIGURE 10-9   An inverted overhead lift.

presenting her partner with a lower back "shelf" for him to lift. That is, he must be able to lift with the heel of his hands under her back, rather than from his hands on her waist. Otherwise, when she is inverted over his head, he will be supporting her weight entirely with his thumbs, which is uncomfortable to say the least. And, of course, he must be supporting her weight at a position close to her center of gravity to allow her to achieve a pleasing line, avoiding rotating back in the direction from which she was lifted or rotating on over his head, which can result in an upside-down head-first dive toward the floor, a distasteful climax to this lift! If his hands are too far up on her back, her legs will tend to be low, and she will not maintain the face-back position over his head. If his hands are too low, she will tend to rotate to a head-down position, which he can no longer control. Of course, she has some range through which she can adjust her body position to control the location of her center of gravity relative to the position of his supporting hands.

Another overhead lift is the "angel lift" shown in figure 10-10, in which the woman arrives over the man's head but front-side–down, with the back arched. In the usual preparation, she runs toward her partner in order to create some momentum that can contribute to the lift (much as a pole vaulter transfers horizontal momentum to vertical momentum in order to clear the bar). He must then lift her with his hands near the front of her hipbones, slowing her forward momentum with an appropriate horizontal force as he lifts and controls her ascent to the overhead position, where she faces the audience while he faces away. Again, if his hands are too high she will fall back in the direction from which she was lifted, while if they are too low she might continue on over his head. In any case, the woman must hold her position with a strong back, or her partner's job becomes impossibly difficult.

The descent from high lifts can be as difficult to control as the ascent. From these overhead lifts, control of the aesthetic line must be maintained by both partners during the descent, a task not easily accomplished at the same time as the necessary slowing of the descent that cushions the landing. From the inverted overhead lift, for instance, there is a strong temptation for the woman to bend forward on descent so that she can see the floor that she is approaching. But in order to maintain the line, she must trust that her partner will place her down gently at just the right moment and position.

FIGURE 10-10  An "angel" lift

## Other Lifts

Some other lifts are worth noting. The "Bluebird" lift is named
for a movement in the "Bluebird" *pas de deux* from *The Sleeping Beauty*. In this lift (to her partner's *right* shoulder, for example) the woman approaches the man face to face, kicks her
left leg in front of her just to her partner's right side, and jumps
up and rotates to a horizontal position front-side-down (as in a
*tour jeté*). She lands on his right shoulder, arching her back so
as to face the audience, as shown in figure 10–11a. Her partner's

*The Mechanics of Lifts*

job is to guide her up to his shoulder with his right hand on her back and his left hand holding her left hand. This lift is quite beautiful, and relatively easy if the timing and take-off motion are correct. But she can easily land on his shoulder with her weight too far forward, tending to fall head first in front of him, or with her weight too far back, in which case she might continue past him and land on her feet in back of him. For the man, the descent is actually harder than the lift, since he must allow her to slide or roll off while supporting her weight with his left hand above and in back of him, or else bend his knees into a deep *plié* or kneel to allow her to step off directly onto her right foot, as shown in figure 10–11 b, c, and d.

In many *pas de deux*, the woman ends sitting on the man's shoulder with one leg bent toward the audience and the other bent down in front of him, both dancers facing the audience, as Benjamin and Julie demonstrate in figure 10–12. In this "shoulder sit" the man lifts the woman by the waist (with her helping by jumping) and places her on his shoulder. One problem that

FIGURE 10–11  The "Bluebird" lift. The last three views show the normal dismount from this lift, which can look awkward if not carried out smoothly.

sometimes occurs in this lift is that the woman waits too long before assuming a sitting configuration, and the man has no horizontal surface that he can put on his shoulder. That is, if her legs remain vertical as he tries to put her on his shoulder, her legs run into his chest, and she ends up "sitting" on his chest rather than his shoulder. He must then lean back and use his hands to push her back against his body to keep her from falling off. The position is not the most graceful!

A shoulder sit can also culminate from a preparation in which the woman runs toward the man, then jumps and turns into a sitting position simultaneously as he lifts and guides her onto his shoulder. Problems in that movement may involve a jump that continues moving horizontally so that he has difficulty getting rid of her traveling momentum, or a misjudgment of landing position so that she misses his shoulder.

Some lifts require a greater degree of strength and coordination from both partners, and are thus more impressive. One is a lift from the ballet *Spring Waters*, choreographed by Asaf Messerer. The woman stands on her right foot with the left bent so its foot is at the right knee. The man, standing behind and to her left, prepares to lift her left ankle with his left hand, while his

FIGURE 10-12  A "shoulder sit" often seen at the end of a *pas de deux*.

right hand is placed at her buttocks so that she can sit on it when aloft. She jumps from her right leg, pushes down with her left leg by straightening it while he lifts that leg, and bends her right leg up, reaching a position supported by his right hand under her right buttock at the top of his straight right arm, left leg extended down vertically. This lift is impressive partly because her head and arms reach a greater height than in any other partnered dance movement.

## Catches

In the lifts described here, the lifter provides at least part of the upward force that elevates the lifted dancer. Catches may involve a jump by one dancer, the other catching her near the highest point in the movement. Such movements appear smoothest when the catch is made exactly at the peak, for two reasons. First, when the jumper is at the peak, the vertical velocity is zero. If that height is maintained after the catch, the trajectory follows a smooth path, since the vertical velocity smoothly approaches zero and then remains zero after the catch. If the catch is made after the descent has begun, the downward motion must be stopped. Second, if the catch is at the peak, the force exerted by the catcher is never greater than the weight of the lifted dancer, whereas if she is caught during descent, he must exert sufficient vertical force not only to support her weight, but also decelerate the descent to a zero vertical velocity. Conversely, if the catch occurs *before* the peak, the free flight phase of the movement is truncated, making it less impressive.

An example of a catch is a "*tour jeté* catch," in which the woman approaches the man face to face, as in the "Bluebird" lift described earlier. She approaches his left side, jumps from her left foot, kicks her right leg up, rotates in the air, then reverses her legs so that her right leg approaches the vertical below her (or bent with the foot at the knee of the left leg), and her left leg is extended to her rear. Her partner catches her with his right hand at her ribs while his left catches her left leg as it rises toward horizontal. When performed smoothly, the movement leaves the impression of a traveling jump with a turn at the peak, suddenly stopping suspended at that highest point. The upward thrust is provided totally by the jumper; the catcher merely stops her vertical motion in mid-air.

## A Final Thrust

The lifts and catches described here represent ways in which a dancer can, with the aid of a partner, create movements far beyond those possible for a solo dancer. Some of the lifts described here are simple straight lifts, in which we can see reasons for technical problems often observed, and reasons for vulnerability to injury associated with these movements. Larger overhead lifts are impressive, but they require careful timing and location of supporting forces in order to produce the image of smoothness and lightness desired. Catches create a different image than lifts; a dancer's expected trajectory through the air is suddenly suspended at its peak through the intervention of a partner.

Moving through the air or hovering several feet off the floor is impressive to perform and to watch. These aesthetic images can be accomplished only by dancers who have the necessary skill, training, strength, and trust in a partner to perform them safely and with a smoothness that belies the effort involved.

# 11

# *The "Black Swan"* Pas de Deux

One of the most famous *pas de deux* in all of dance occurs in the third act of the ballet *Swan Lake.* The best-known original choreography for this ballet was by Marius Petipa and Lev Ivanov for a production first performed in St. Petersburg in 1895. Since that time most ballerinas have aspired to dance the double role of Odette-Odile, which requires not only excellent technique, but an ability to portray two very different personalities.

## *Swan Lake*—The Context for the "Black Swan" *Pas de deux*

The ballet, in four acts, revolves around Siegfried, a prince of marrying age. While hunting by a lake one evening, Siegfried comes across Odette, a beautiful woman at night, but doomed by the spell of an evil magician to become a swan at sunrise each day. Siegfried falls in love with Odette, who explains to him that

FIGURE 11-1 Julie Kent with Guillaume Graffin in American Ballet Theatre's *Swan Lake.*

the spell will be broken if the man who loves her swears his eternal love to her and does not betray her. Siegfried willingly pledges his love to her, and invites her to a celebration at his castle the following night to be introduced as his betrothed.

Act III of the ballet is Siegfried's birthday party, at which he is to select his future bride from among the most beautiful and eligible maidens. He is delighted when he seems to see Odette arriving with the evil magician Von Rothbart. But he doesn't realize that she is not Odette but Odile, an imposter brought to the gathering by Von Rothbart in order to trick Siegfried into betraying Odette. Odette embodies innocence, purity, kindness, and goodness. The imposter, Odile, epitomizes the opposite; she is mysterious, alluring, manipulative, and evil. Her job is to deceive Siegfried, causing him to swear his love to her rather than to the real Odette. The dance of Odile and Siegfried is the famous "Black Swan" *pas de deux*, so called because Odile is dressed in black, contrasting with the pure white of the swan/woman Odette.

The "Black Swan" *pas de deux* is the dance of an infatuated Siegfried with the cunning woman he thinks is Odette. The way the dancers meet the challenge of characterizing these roles is one of the most appealing aspects of this ballet, and particularly of this *pas de deux*. The ballerina's challenge is to make it clear to the audience that she is really the evil Odile, while making her impersonation of Odette, intended to deceive Siegfried, believable as well.

Later in Act III, Siegfried does swear his love for the woman he believes to be Odette, dooming Odette to her fate. Siegfried realizes his tragic mistake, and leaves to try to find Odette. In Act IV, he does indeed find her by the lake, and pleads for her forgiveness. She, having forgiven Siegfried, knows that she can now break the spell only by sacrificing herself. Siegfried, wishing to be with her at all costs, joins her as they both throw themselves to the mercy of the lake and to eternity.

Cynthia speaking: "In the *pas de deux* there must be a sense of excitement by the prince, who believes he has met the woman who will be his wife and the future princess. And all the while, Odile keeps up the game of trying to convince him that she is Odette. It is important, of course, to execute the steps as well as possible, but in addition, the story line is crucially important. A great ballerina will play with the musicality by speeding up or slowing down her movements while fitting them into

*The "Black Swan"* Pas de Deux

the musical phrase. She must be careful not to be so much like Odette in movement quality that the audience is not convinced that she's Odile, and yet enough so that Siegfried doesn't catch on that she's an imposter. The responsibility of the artists is to convince everyone of their roles, and the difficulty is to balance just the right amounts of subtlety and clarity." (The quoted comments reflect my [CH's] experience in dancing this *pas de deux* many times with American Ballet Theatre and the Royal Ballet of Great Britain.)

## The "Black Swan" *Pas de deux*

Although the vivid portrayal of the individual characters is important in the "Black Swan" *pas de deux*, there is also an intriguing sequence of dance movements that represent the interactions between Siegfried and Odile. The following description applies to the example of this *pas de deux* reproduced on the accompanying video cassette, staged by Natalia Makarova and danced by Evelyn Hart and Peter Schaufuss with the London Festival Ballet. The discussion that follows includes a hint of what might be going through the minds of the performers in addition to an analysis of some of the physical processes that are occurring during the interaction between the two dancers.

The first sequence of steps moves from stage right to stage left, and is often danced by Odile and Siegfried after she has been introduced to the queen. In this version, Odile is partnered in the first sequence by Von Rothbart as he brings Odile to meet the queen. The steps involved are a *pas de bourrée couru* (running steps *en pointe*) to a brush of the right leg into *altitude derrière*. Then a *tombé* out of that into a lift is followed by a scissors movement of her legs in front. During this lift the man takes a few steps forward before placing Odile down again.

Cynthia: "And I usually have to try to give my partner a bit of a shelf in my upper back for his hands, enabling him to get under me enough so that we can travel forward while I scissor my legs in the air. I usually start the sequence by moving as broadly as possible, not attacking each movement too sharply. The movement occurs three times, after which I turn back toward stage right. Siegfried then joins me for a traveling lift moving toward stage right.

"The next sequence is also performed three times, and involves a tricky lift that is like a *glissade* in the air." (Figure 11-2

FIGURE 11-2 A traveling lift that appears early in the "Black Swan" *pas de deux,* and demonstrates the challenge to the lifter to keep his partner moving in a smooth trajectory despite the rise and fall of her legs during the lift (video cassette frame).

is a "reminder" frame from the video cassette showing that lift, which begins at 0:16 on the cassette.) "That is, I push off with the right leg leaving the ground first, and then he quickly lifts me sideways so that I can lift the left leg to the side in a symmetrical position—almost a split position. This involves the man lifting the ballerina higher just as her head and torso tend to come down. So the lift, supported at the waist, must be perfectly timed." The difficulty in carrying out that lift smoothly arises because Siegfried should not apply an even vertical lifting force that would cause Odile's center of gravity to rise evenly. When her legs rise into second position, her center of gravity rises relative to her body (perhaps from the lower abdomen to the stomach). If that movement happens too quickly, her torso and head may actually drop just when they should be approaching the peak of the lift. Her partner must therefore exert a greater lifting force as her legs rise so that her torso and head can continue to rise while the center of gravity is going up *more rapidly.* The opposite effect occurs on the descent, in which she must wait until her center of gravity is descending until she lowers her legs, so that her torso and head do not react by moving upward when she should be descending.

Cynthia: "Next I step further side, and fold myself like a bird covering herself with her wings, while raising my right leg to my left knee and then extending it to the side. An *en dedans pirouette* follows, in which Siegfried exerts a torque on my waist while I store some rotational momentum in my right leg as it starts rotating toward the front. He doesn't need much force, as this is only a single turn, which I then finish in *arabesque*, facing left. I often think of helping him stop the rotation by rapidly extending my leg to *arabesque*, and keeping my focus to the front, or to the audience. This change from turning to focusing gives me a dynamic sharpness."

After a few moments of separation, the two dancers come together for another series of lifts while moving from stage left toward stage right (beginning at 0:49 on the recording). Siegfried lifts with his left hand at her right hip while she is facing him, and uses his right hand with hers as a guide to steady the lift. The lift is not extended in duration, as her center of gravity is well away from his support at the floor, and he cannot therefore exert a lifting force as great as her weight. The "lift" is more an "aided jump." Both partners must assure that her center of gravity is directly above his supporting hand, or else she will be rotated forward, backward, or sideways by the torque resulting from his lifting force and the downward force of gravity, or will be linearly accelerated away from the desired location. The woman helps produce a smooth movement by assuring that her body is configured such that her center of gravity is directly over a horizontal "shelf" at her hip. Her partner must then assure that his hand is placed correctly on her hip, although small discrepancies can be corrected by means of his other hand in contact with hers.

Cynthia: "There are several ways I have done this lift. Whatever the positioning of the man's hands, the most important thing for me to remember is to turn my left shoulder quickly to the front in the *fouetté*, or the flip, as soon as possible. I have done the *fouetté attitude* with no actual boost from my partner except sometimes just the resistance of his hands. Or I have done it with our right hands interconnected, and he scoops me into the air by placing his right hand at a low place on my right hip, and his left arm swings up to the fifth position alone."

The waltz section of the *pas de deux* ends with Odile's series of *piqué* turns ending in an *en dehors pirouette* to a position with her back to the audience but arched over to face them, supported by Siegfried's hands at her waist. (This moment occurs at 1:18; that frame is reproduced in figure 11-3.) The slow *adagio* section of the *pas de deux* begins here with an extended violin solo.

Following a slow turn in *attitude derrière*, Odile descends into a *penchée* supported only by Siegfried's right hand at her

FIGURE 11-3 The final pose from a supported *pirouette* at the end of the waltz section of the *pas de deux,* which precedes the slow adagio section (video cassette frame).

waist. How can Siegfried control her position with just the one hand during the following *promenade*? Clearly, either he must be gripping her waist with his hand or she must be slightly off balance so that her weight is leaning somewhat in to him. Otherwise he could exert no force on her, and thus would have no control over her position and could not aid her balance or cause her to turn. Too much lean makes it difficult to maintain balance while turning, so he actually compromises, with some of her weight leaning against his hand and some control coming from a slight grip of her waist with his hand.

Odile (at 1:54) performs an *arabesque penchée* supported at the waist by Siegfried. In this supported pose a woman wants to be held in a position as comfortable as possible so that she can hold a pleasing *arabesque* line. As described in chapter 8, the position she finds comfortable depends on the arch of her foot. If she has relatively little arch, a balanced position in which her center of gravity is directly above her supporting toe would be uncomfortable, since she would have to be exerting a torque in the ankle in order to keep herself up on *pointe*. If her arch is greater, then the toe end of her foot can be in a straight line along her leg and under her center of gravity, allowing her to be comfortable in a balanced position, since little torque in the ankle is required. If she holds an *arabesque* position alone, she does not have the luxury of being able to hold the position off balance, but a partner can provide the forces necessary to hold her there. As seen here, Ms. Hart has an excellent arch, allowing her to be comfortable while being held very close to balance.

At 2:30 on the video cassette, the two dancers move to stage right, where Siegfried fits in behind Odile's *arabesque* and allows her to fall forward by lunging forward himself and holding her waist with his right arm. In that moment there is a tendency for Siegfried's horizontal force, necessary to stop Odile's forward travel, to cause her to slip backward. The force must be just enough to stop her and bring her back upright without causing her to slip. Clearly, a large part of the total force he exerts must be a vertical supporting force that supports her weight and starts her return to an upright position, rather than a horizontal force, which could succeed in bringing her back up but could also cause her to slip.

She then rests her right arm over Siegfried's right arm as he brings her upright again, and still using his arm as support, she rolls off *pointe* and turns to a stable position.

A short while later, Odile runs to an *arabesque* supported by her right hand in contact with Siegfried's right hand, with him standing behind her. Odile starts a *pirouette* in a way that seems easy, but is actually rather tricky. (This movement begins at 3:01, and is shown in the video frame reproduced in figure 11-4.) With only her right hand in contact with his, and positioned in *arabesque*, she starts an *en dedans pirouette* to the

FIGURE 11-4   The beginning of an *en dedans pirouette* from *arabesque*. The forces required for the turn can destroy Evelyn's balance if she does not compensate in some way (video cassette frame).

*The "Black Swan"* Pas de Deux

*161*

right, on her right supporting leg. What is the source of the torque that starts her turning? Her right hand must be displaced from the vertical axis of rotation, or no torque is possible. But then if she exerts a force against his hand directed toward her left, she will not only start the turn in the desired direction, but will also experience a net force pushing her to her right. This force will necessarily destroy her balance *unless* she is off balance toward her left to begin with, and the applied force just returns her to a balance position as the *pirouette* starts. The challenge for her is to adjust her balance and the magnitude of her force so that the turn begins with the music, has the right duration, and allows her to remain balanced until her partner's hands can move to her waist to help her balance. To accomplish that move takes much experience and sensitivity to her partner's way of moving and the solidity with which he holds his hand. The turn finishes in *arabesque*, so after the push for the turn, Siegfried moves to a position behind Odile while keeping his hands around her waist in order to stop her in *arabesque*.

Cynthia: "This turn gives most dancers problems, as it is a delicate action. The trouble I've found is that the man usually has more strength in his arms than the woman, and the tendency is for me to fall to my left (toward the audience), even though he is pushing to my right. The tendency to overcompensate can be quite strong! I've taken force for five or six turns and ended up only down to two, which is rather embarrassing."

Odile soon moves to an *arabesque* with arms high (at 3:12) facing the audience, balancing by means of contact between her right hand and the right hand of her partner, who is standing to her right side with his back to the audience. She must now perform a little more than two slow turns under his hand while in *attitude penchée*, which requires not only a finely tuned sense of balance, but also a control of the twisting torque exerted by her hand against his that enables her to control that slow turn. After she joins both hands with his for a promenade, she extends her leg into *attitude derrière* with her right leg circled behind him, descends into a *penchée*, recovers, and performs a supported *fouetté* finger turn. (The beginning of that turn occurs at 3:25, and is shown in figure 11-5.) A similar movement was discussed in chapter 6. Note that she pushes off with her left hand against his; that is the source of the torque. The axis of rotation is determined by her supporting foot at the floor and his hand over her head. His finger provides a vertical "axle" on

FIGURE 11-5  The beginning of a "finger turn." The torque for the turn comes from the left hand contact; the rotational momentum is stored in the rotating leg until sufficient momentum has been acquired for the turn rate desired (video cassette frame).

which her hand can rotate. Now if she were in a constant position as she pushed off, she would gain an insufficient amount of rotational momentum. So she moves her leg from front to side while she is pushing against his hand, thus storing rotational momentum while the torque is still being exerted by his left hand against hers. The final rotational momentum she achieves for the turn is thereby made sufficient for the rate of turn desired.

A *rond de jambe* with her working leg ends that phase of the movement, after which the two again separate. At this point (3:31), Von Rothbart rushes in to shield Siegfried from seeing the real Odette, with whom Siegfried thinks he is dancing. (Cynthia: "This break in Odile's action happens just as her supporting leg feels like lead from being *en pointe* through much of the previous movement!") Odette has appeared in a window to plead with Siegfried to keep his promise to her that he will love no one but her. But Siegfried is preoccupied with his fascination with Odile; he is blind to Odette's pleas. (In most live productions, the "vision" of Odette has to be another dancer impersonating her.)

Later, Odile is pulled up off the floor by Siegfried, and steps into a low *arabesque*. His hands contact hers over her head and help her establish balance, after which he steps back and leaves her balanced alone for several breathless moments (around 4:20, and shown in figure 11-6). Cynthia: "I found that if the prince placed my hands so that the arms are in symmetric positions, not too far forward or back, then I could balance. Otherwise, during

The *"Black Swan"* Pas de Deux

*163*

FIGURE 11-6   An extended balance maintained by Evelyn for several seconds (video cassette frame).

the attempt to balance, I would have to make an adjustment with my arms, and that movement could easily throw off my placement, and I'd go right off balance."

There follows a promenade in *arabesque penchée* with support from just his right hand. What causes the turn? As in an earlier similar movement, he must be using his hand alone in order to cause the torque that produces the rotation, but must not in the process throw her off balance.

Shortly after an almost triumphant look from Odile to a smiling queen, she returns to stand next to Siegfried, slowly bringing her left leg up into a high second position extension to the side (at 4:51). She turns to face her partner, brings her left leg down, and shifts her weight to that leg as she starts an *en dehors pirouette* to the right on her left leg with her right in a *passé*

FIGURE 11-7   The final pose in the "Black Swan" *pas de deux* (video cassette frame).

*The "Black Swan"* Pas de Deux

164

position. Where does the torque come from for that turn? Her right hand does have contact with his left hand at a location displaced from her axis of rotation, so a force there will help start the turn. But as happened before, such a force will not only start a turn, but will also tend to move her body laterally. Therefore she must adjust her balance so as not to throw herself off in that process. But she also has both feet on the floor for a short time, and can exert some torque with her feet during that time. If the timing is a bit different, momentum can be stored in the leg and arms as the push-off from Siegfried's hand occurs, rather than using two feet at the floor for some of the torque.

The end of the *pas de deux* occurs when Odile finishes this last turn in *arabesque* facing stage left, then steps down to a reversed *arabesque* facing stage right. Siegfried kneels while supporting her waist, and she bends back with her leg raised in *attitude*. This final pose of the *pas de deux* (shown in figure 11-7) shows a swanlike image of a triumphant Odile, with Siegfried kneeling submissively at her feet.

# 12

# *Ice Skating*

Figure skating is often considered a form of dance. The aims of skating may be different from those of stage dancing, in that this activity has evolved as a competitive sport in which the degree of difficulty of the moves is as important as their aesthetic quality in the evaluation of judges. In fact, skaters can sometimes score well in a competition even if they falter seriously in carrying out difficult moves. There are also some movements that are "required" for competition, so the choreography is sometimes constrained. But exhibition skating outside of the competitive realm remains primarily a dance-based art form. And the aesthetic component is never absent in figure skating or partnered skating, so analyses similar to those applied to dance can be appropriate and useful.

There are, of course, physical differences between dancing on a stage and skating on ice—differences that are intriguing and worth identifying and analyzing. Perhaps the most obvious difference is that skaters are almost always moving at a significant speed over the ice as they perform their movements, often making those movements quite spectacular merely because of their speed.

FIGURE 12-1   Renée Roca and Donald Adair. (Photo by Paul Harvath.)

As in dance, some of the most intriguing applications of physical principles are those for skaters moving while interacting as partners. Ice dancing and pairs skating both involve ice skating with a partner and have many similarities to dancing with a partner on a stage floor. There are poses, turns, and lifts that can be seen, appreciated, and analyzed in ways described in earlier chapters. In partnered ice skating there is usually the traditional male–female role differentiation in that the male does the lifting and supporting of the female, but in solo skating the woman skater is more likely than the woman dancer to be very athletic and carry out moves that are similar or identical to those of her male counterpart.

## Physical Differences Between Skating and Dance

Let us note some physical differences between skating and stage dancing that have implications for the kind of movements involved. Compared to a dancer, a skater moves with very small friction along the longitudinal axis of the skate, and very large friction perpendicular to that axis. The differences are profound. For instance, a skater can move at almost constant speed over the surface without moving any part of the body. A dancer, in order to move linearly, must walk or run, involving very dynamic movements of the body. Second, skaters can develop very high velocities compared to those attainable by dancers, since speed can be continuously gained by repeatedly pushing against the ice surface while little momentum is lost through friction. And because skaters' velocities are much greater, preventing as rapid changes in direction as can occur on a stage floor, the surface on which they skate is usually much larger than a typical stage. Third, skaters are as often moving backward as forward, creating an entirely different realm of movements that can be initiated from that state of motion. Fourth, skaters do perform *pirouettes*, which they call "spins," but these turns usually allow the skate on the supporting foot to revolve in a small circular arc rather than turning on the skate itself, thereby preventing any part of the skate blade from having to move perpendicular to its longitudinal axis. The fact that the rotation axis of a skater is usually displaced from the part of the skate in contact with the ice is not as important to the observer as other differences, but *is* significant in the physical properties of the rotation.

How do ice skaters use these differences? Merely the fact that skaters move so fast adds to the impressiveness of the movements, but that speed also gives them some physical advantages over stage dancers. How are these larger velocities used?

## Balance and Poses

Consider first balance and poses, as analyzed for dancers in chapters 2 and 8. The most noticeable aesthetic difference that distinguishes skating is that a pose can be held with constant body configuration, but the linear movement over the ice produces a dynamic effect very different from the static positions of dancers in motionless poses. The eye of the observer can follow movement while seeing the unchanging line of the bodies presented over some duration of time. *Dancers* holding a fixed pose for any length of time create an image that stagnates very quickly. However, skaters do experience some friction, which means that the body positions held when moving are slightly different than when stationary. For instance, in an *arabesque* position, the supporting leg must be angled forward into the direction of motion in order to avoid toppling forward due to the small but

FIGURE 12-2   Kristi Yamaguchi balanced in a moving *arabesque penché*. (Photo by Paul Harvath.)

important force of friction on that supporting foot. Often an image of dynamic motion is created even in a still photograph of a moving skater.

Although similar in many ways, the roles of the two skating partners can be subtly different from those of dancing partners. In dance, the male is often responsible for helping his partner maintain balance, and if she tries to adjust her own balance, his job is made harder. Ice dancers, however, are almost always moving, allowing their point of contact at the surface to be constantly changing relative to the position of the other skater. Small changes in the orientation of the skate can substantially change the position of that point of contact and the distance from the partner, thus changing the body configuration and the condition of balance. Both partners, therefore, must take an active role in maintaining balance. If the two partners are in contact while moving, their skates must be absolutely parallel, or else the distance between them will vary as they move.

How is the skate different from the foot of a dancer? First, the foot is flexible, so that contact with the floor can be made by the entire length of the foot, just the ball of the foot and the toes, or, in the case of *pointe* shoes, just the small "box" end of the shoe. Balance is clearly harder the smaller the area of contact with the floor. The skate, on the other hand, is rigid and slightly convex. A small portion of the length of the skate is actually in contact with the ice, but the foot can be "rocked" forward or backward, allowing the location of the region of contact to be shifted forward or backward as necessary to maintain balance.

Now, suppose the skater is moving forward on one skate and becomes slightly off balance toward the front, in the direction of motion. Balance can be corrected by rocking forward on the skate so that the region of contact moves forward, but rocking too far forward may cause the toe pick—the toothed front edge of the blade—to grab the ice, causing an uncontrolled fall forward. Notice that skating backward avoids that problem, as there is no comparable "heel pick" at the rear end of the skate blade that would cause a fall backward, in the direction of motion. And rocking forward (while skating backward) to prevent a fall forward would actually help prevent the fall by increasing the friction force in a direction that counteracts the toppling motion. (Engineers would identify this situation as "negative feedback," as opposed to the "positive feedback" that contributed to the fall when one was skating forward.)

# Rotations Around the Body's Vertical Axis

Rotations, as described in chapters 4 and 9 for dancers, are an important part of skating as well. First, note that the terminology is different for skaters than for dancers. To skaters, who are almost always moving linearly, a "turn" represents a change in the orientation of the body relative to the direction of motion. Turns involve quick reversals of the axis of the skate from skating forward to backward, or vice versa, usually with little change in the direction or magnitude of the linear momentum. A "spin" is what a dancer would identify as a *pirouette*, a *tour en l'air*, or another rotation of the body around a vertical axis.

Partnered spins may involve *pirouettes*, although the skating partner does not often "support" a spin in the same way a dancing partner does. There are spins in the air, either from jumps for a solo skater, or partner-aided jumps or throws. There are rotations involving swinging around a partner, or two partners swinging around a common axis between them. One obvious question is why skaters seem able to maintain their balance

FIGURE 12-4 Tonya Harding in a spin. Unlike a dancer performing a *pirouette*, the supporting foot of a skater moves in a small circle around the axis of rotation. (Photo by Paul Harvath.)

while spinning for a far longer time than dancers do. There are two answers. First, and most important, a skater's foot usually revolves in a small circular arc around a central vertical axis of rotation, thereby effectively increasing the size of the area of support at the surface. As long as the skater's center of gravity remains on a vertical line that passes through this circular area of support, balance can be maintained. And whereas a dancer would have to hop to change the location of the contact area at the floor, a skater, because the skate is moving, can change the location of that contact area quite readily. Second, when a skater spins at perhaps three or more revolutions per second, the rotation rate is large enough that there begins to be a gyroscopic effect that allows an off-balance spinning skater to precess rather than topple. That is, the axis of rotation has some tendency to sweep out a cone-shaped path around the vertical (with the apex of the cone at the point of contact with the ice), much as a spinning top does as it slows down. A top takes awhile to slow to the point of toppling over, even if it is pushed off balance while it is rotating.

## Rotations Around a Vertical Axis Displaced from the Body

Movements are often seen in which the man swings the woman around him in a circular path, holding her by the hands while the rest of her body is extended toward the outside of the circle. An example is the "death spiral," in which the woman's body, and her head in particular, is quite close to the ice while she is swung in a circular path by her partner. In that case most of the centripetal force (the inward force that maintains her circular motion) comes from the man's hands, but some can come also from the woman's skates in contact with the ice. That is, if the man lets go, his partner will not be able to continue in the tight circular path, although some curvature is possible just from the lateral force of the ice against her skates, directed toward the inside of the circle.

A numerical example demonstrates the physical principles that apply to the death spiral. Suppose the woman is revolving in a circular path made by her skates at a rate of one revolution every two seconds and that the radius of the circular path is about 9 feet (or 2.7 meters). For a woman 5′ 3″ tall with her arms

FIGURE 12-5   Jill Watson and Peter Oppegard perform a "death spiral." The angle of the body with the horizontal, and the forces required to maintain this position while moving in a circular path, are discussed in the accompanying text. (Photo by Paul Harvath.)

outstretched above her, her center of gravity is about 3′ 8″ above her feet. If she depends totally on the forces at her skates to keep her moving in a circular path and to support her weight, the angle between the line of her body and the horizontal would be about 37°. But the death spiral is often carried out with an angle considerably less than 37°, and thus she would fall to the surface. Looked at another way, suppose the angle between her body and the horizontal is 10°. How fast would she have to be revolving in a circular path in order to be in equilibrium for that motion and not fall to the ice? Calculations show that she would be moving at almost one revolution per second, and the horizontal force between her skates and the ice would be more than 570 pounds!

Since the death spiral requires a vertical force from the partner to help keep the skater from falling, she has supporting forces at two locations—her feet, and her hands over her head. The challenge to her is to keep her body arched so that she doesn't "droop" in the middle between the two support points.

*Ice Skating*

FIGURE 12-6 A vertical throw with spin performed by Katie Keely and Joe Mero. The mechanism for acquiring the substantial rotational momentum in this movement involves torques from both the lifter and the spinner. (Photo by Paul Harvath.)

## Rotations Around a Vertical Axis Aloft

A common and impressive movement in solo skating and partnered skating is a jump or throw in the air with a rotation of perhaps three full revolutions before landing, as in a salchow, for instance. How do skaters gain the necessary rotational momentum for such a rapid turn, and how do they get rid of the rotational momentum upon landing? Gaining the rotational momentum can involve the same mechanisms used by dancers to initiate turns, namely, exerting equal and opposite forces with the two feet against the surface with some distance between the lines of action of the forces, for some length of time, or by twisting with one foot against the surface (usually the latter, for skaters). A dancer in a normal preparation position for a *pirouette* orients the feet in such a way that forces between the foot and the floor are exerted in a direction parallel to the longitudinal axis of the foot. Clearly, since that direction is along the axis of the skate, a skater cannot exert forces in that way. That is why skaters start spins by twisting with one foot against the ice while storing rotational momentum in the rest of the body, including the free leg, before bringing that leg in close to the body and developing a large rotational velocity.

In the case of a throw by a partner, the woman gains rotational momentum not only from the mechanisms described above, but also from the forces exerted by her partner's hands as he is lifting her.

How much rotational momentum is acquired in these processes that initiate turns in the air? Measurements show that the skater is in the air about one second during a triple turn from a throw by a partner, so her rate of rotation is about 3.0 revolutions per second. If she holds her arms close to the body and her legs are close together, her rotational inertia is perhaps .35 kg-m$^2$. Therefore she has a rotational momentum of about 1.0 kg-m$^2$/s.

Now, how does the skater get rid of that rotational momentum when she wants to land and has to stop the rotation rather quickly in order to continue a linear movement across the ice? When she lands on the supporting leg, the other leg swings through an arc while the skate on the supporting leg exerts a twisting torque against the ice in order to destroy the rotational momentum of the turn. If that rotating leg makes an angle of 30° with the horizontal as it rotates around an axis through the hip joint, it has a rotational inertia of about 1.0 kg-m$^2$ and thus rotates at about one revolution per second, or one third the rate of the full body rotation while in the air, while the rest of the body stops its rotation totally. And of course the leg would slow its rotation as the rotational momentum is destroyed. Assuming that the leg moves through an angle of about 180° while slowing uniformly, that process of slowing would take about one second. During that time the skater, whose body (except for the rotating leg) has ceased rotating, can maintain the orientation that allows her to continue her linear movement along the ice.

## Vertical Jumps

Consider now the process involved in skating jumps and lifts. Many aspects of these movements are similar to those observed in dance, as described in chapters 3 and 10, but again the horizontal motion has important implications. Can skaters use the fact that they are in rapid linear motion to increase the height to which they can jump or be thrown? There is a mechanism familiar to pole vaulters and high jumpers that allows horizontal momentum to be converted to vertical momentum. That momentum allows skaters to use their greater speed in order to jump higher.

Let's look at the process more closely. Suppose a pole vaulter moving with some speed plants the pole on the ground in front of him. Since his center of gravity is moving horizontally some distance above the ground, there is a rotational momentum around the end of the pole that is in contact with the ground. If the body is prevented from changing its radial distance from that contact point, rotational momentum will be conserved only by a shift in the direction of the body's motion from horizontal to a direction perpendicular to the radius from the body to the contact, or pivot, point. Since that motion now has a vertical component, some of the horizontal momentum has been converted to vertical momentum.

A pole vaulter does many other things in the process of maximizing his height, such as jumping vertically at the time he starts to use the pole to convert his horizontal momentum to vertical. He also uses his arms to increase the radial distance from the contact point on the ground to his center of gravity (to "climb" the pole and push off from it) as he approaches the peak of the motion. And, of course, he is swinging his body from the point of contact between the hands and the pole in order to cause a more gradual conversion of horizontal to vertical momentum. This allows the loss of mechanical energy in the process to be minimized. The bending fiberglass pole also smooths that conversion process. But the fundamental principle is that of converting horizontal momentum to vertical momentum.

A high jumper accomplishes the same thing, but in a more subtle way. A high jumper can jump higher with a running start than from a standing position because of that transfer from horizontal to vertical momentum. In that case the jumper uses the take-off leg in the same way the vaulter uses the pole, but also stores vertical momentum as the free leg rotates upward.

How does a skater use this principle? With the greater horizontal momentum that accompanies the greater speed, the skater must plant one skate in such a way that it stops temporarily, so that the horizontal momentum can be converted to vertical by a process similar to that described above. As the skater takes off from one leg, the free leg swings up around a pivot axis at the hip much as the entire mass of the pole vaulter's body swings up from the pivot at the hand contact on the pole. When the leg is moving vertically, the skater transfers its vertical momentum to the body as a whole.

Note that skaters' jumps almost always involve spins at the same time, making all of these processes physically complicated. Most jumps (loops, toe loops, salchows, flips, and lutzes, for instance) begin while one is skating backward. The axel occurs from a forward motion. Since all jumps end moving backward, most involve integral numbers of rotations—1, 2, 3, or 4 spins in the air. The axel involves rotations of $1\frac{1}{2}$, $2\frac{1}{2}$, or $3\frac{1}{2}$ turns. The ending movement described above, which gets rid of the rotational momentum of the spin, involves bringing the free leg forward upon landing, then slowing it as it rotates to the rear to a low *arabesque* position extended toward the direction of motion.

How can skaters do triple and quadruple spins in the air while dancers *sometimes* perform a double *tour en l'air* well? There are two answers. First, because of the rapid linear motion, greater height is possible for skaters than for dancers, allowing them more time to complete the spins. (Note, however, that the same reasoning used in chapter 3 on vertical jumps tells us that an increase in height of 20 percent increases the time aloft by less than 10 percent!) Second, the higher-order spinning jumps in skating are often accomplished with a sacrifice in aesthetic appearance, since physical constraints may make such compromises necessary in order for the movement to be possible at all. The preparation positions may be less than pleasing, for instance. Since the aesthetic appearance is not the *only* consideration in skating, such sacrifices are acceptable. The skater's body position while spinning is as compact along the rotation axis as possible, allowing for a large rate of rotation for a modest rotational momentum. One resulting challenge that skaters face is that the large centrifugal force makes holding the arms and legs close to the body very difficult.

## Vertical Lifts

When ice skaters are performing with partners, the height and ease of lifts is quite notable. When the woman is lifted, she often aids that lift through her own jump, which can be stronger if she applies the techniques described earlier for using the linear momentum from her horizontal motion.

Ice dancers can take advantage of the fact that they are in linear motion during their movements. Their landings from lifts are usually moving landings, in which the woman must assure that her skates are oriented in the direction of movement when landing, allowing her to continue moving without having to run or walk in order to do so, as is the case when one is dancing on a stage. Landings from lifts can also involve subsequent rotations around the partner.

Some ice skating lifts, such as the "star" lift, are extended for some duration in the air. As in dance, the lifting partner must hold her aloft with the point of contact at his hands directly over his area of support at the ice in order to avoid large torques caused by her center of gravity being displaced horizontally from his support. That is, her center of gravity should be on a vertical line at or above his hands, and directly above his shoulders and feet. Note, however, that he is holding his partner aloft while maintaining his own balance, despite being on a surface that is highly slippery in the longitudinal direction of his skate blades. That is a feat of control of a kind dancers never have to perform!

The lack of friction in the fore/aft direction for skaters has another consequence in lifts. A *dancer* lifting his partner by her back to an overhead position often pushes forward early in the lift in order to use the friction between his hands and her body in order to provide some of the upward force—a force tangential to her body, or vertical when her back is oriented vertically. Later in the lift her back approaches the horizontal, and a force tangential to her back is no longer necessary. For skaters, the lack of forward friction at the surface makes it very difficult to exert that forward force early in the lifting process. The man would merely be pushing his partner away from him. The partners must find other means to cause the woman's center of gravity to start rising.

FIGURE 12-7  Natasha Kuchiki and Todd Sand perform a star lift. It is difficult for the lifter to control the position of his partner and keep her center of gravity directly over his support at the ice while he is moving. (Photo by Paul Harvath.)

*Ice Skating*

*179*

FIGURE 12-8 Brian Boitano leaning into a circular path. (Photo by Paul Harvath.)

## A Final Glide

The interaction between partners, whether in dance or in ice skating, requires the same respect, sensitivity, and musicality. But dancers have a normal frictional interaction with the floor on which they stand, walk, glide, or run, while ice skaters have a profoundly different interaction with the surface. Their dance-type movements can occur while they are in rapid linear motion forward or backward, and they can use that momentum to their advantage either to increase the height of the jumps and lifts or to contribute to the rotational motion in spins on the surface or in the air. The results create an image that adds some dynamic qualities, while perhaps sacrificing other qualities such as lyricism. The appeal to audiences is different in some ways, and similar in others.

What may dancers find disconcerting about skating? First, there is a strong appeal, particularly in classical ballet, to the pointed foot, that allows the line of the leg to be continued down to the toes. The skate adds an object at the end of the leg more or less perpendicular to its length, producing an abrupt end to the continuous line. An observer who is accustomed to dance must overcome a tendency to find that object on the leg detracting from an otherwise graceful line. On the other hand, those accustomed to watching skaters accomplish three or three-and-a-half turns in the air are less impressed with dancers who can barely accomplish two turns comfortably. Why are dancers constrained to try to initiate a *tour en l'air* with the feet close together, thereby sacrificing the torque that would be possible if the feet started farther apart? An observer of dance might feel that skaters occupy much of their time just building up speed and position in preparation for a brief jump or lift—perhaps seen as long transitions between those brief "events"—whereas an observer of skating might miss those sudden accents, wondering why dance seems to be more seamless, with transitions melding into identifiable movements.

Despite the differences, dance observers and skating enthusiasts have much in common to appreciate in these two related art forms.

# 13

# *A Step into the Future*

What will dancers be doing in fifty years? In many fields of human activity, including science and the arts, there are those who feel that the remaining opportunities for creative innovation are limited—that everything interesting that can be done already has been done. Where are innovations still occurring in science? What roles do science and technology play in the continuing evolution of the arts?

In science, true advances are increasingly difficult. As understanding of nature is sought at deeper and deeper levels, the instruments necessary for advancement become larger and larger, and increasingly expensive. The superconducting supercollider is an example. In order to investigate the tiniest and most fundamental building blocks of all matter, the instrument necessary for the investigation requires an area equal to that of a large city, and is built at the cost of many billions of dollars. How much progress toward understanding nature can society

FIGURE 13-1   Young students at the Dance Theatre of Harlem.

afford? (In fact, funding for the superconducting supercollider was ended by action of Congress late in 1993, an action perhaps based more on politics than philosophy.) Currently most research represents small increments of advance in the total body of knowledge. There are exceptions, of course. Chaos theory is providing new insights into the most complex aspects of nature, such as the weather. It is an active area of research now, made possible largely because of computers, and characterized by relatively low cost.

In music, major innovations no longer seem possible within the traditional context of simple and straightforward harmonic, melodic, and rhythmic structures with which Western ears are familiar. Advances in music composition have involved more and more extensive departures from the easily understood and appreciated structures. But progress in music also occurs through the use of technology. Electronics and computer technology have provided both composers and performers with tools that were beyond the wildest dreams of musicians even a few decades ago. The range of tones, combinations, rhythms, and structures accessible to musicians is now limited only by the ability of the human ear to perceive.

What are the constraints on the future evolution of human physical activity such as dance and athletics? Are there ways in which science and technology might alleviate those constraints as they have for music? One cannot avoid the fact that the fundamental instrument of dance and athletics is the human body, which cannot be changed in major ways by technical means. It is true that an understanding of anatomy can help dancers and athletes maximize the effectiveness with which their bodies perform the range of movements called for. Sports medicine is a mature field. Those in the medical profession, including physical therapists, are now taking dancers and their problems quite seriously, developing techniques for dealing with the unique problems and pressures dancers face.

Athletes, like dancers, continually strive to maximize the effectiveness of their performance. Sometimes technology contributes a major advance, such as the invention of the fiberglass pole-vault pole. Occasionally a fundamentally new technique for an athletic activity is invented, such as the Fosbury "flop" for the high jump. But in this case also, a technological advance—the air bag used to cushion the landing—made that new high jump technique feasible.

How is technology contributing to the advancement of dance? The development of systems for notating and recording dance for historical and archival purposes complements innovation in the creation of dance. These systems allow for otherwise ephemeral dances to be retained for the future. Such archives are necessary, since newness is empty without the record of tradition from which it grows. It is also true that computer simulations are beginning to help choreographers develop their craft efficiently, without the need to have live dancers available throughout their experimentation.

Technology can be a tool for making choreographers' and dancers' jobs easier. Science, on the other hand, produces new and deeper levels of understanding of the activity of dance itself. There is a great need for people from both the science world and the dance arena to build bridges between those areas. In that way there can be growth in the contributions that science can make to dance. Scientists need to grasp the context in which their science can be useful; people in the dance world must be open to the value of the understanding that science can provide. The benefits of the cross-fertilization of ideas between these traditionally disparate fields can be enormous.

Ultimately dance remains an aesthetic communication between a dancer and an observer through the medium of the dancer's body. But the natural structure of physical law is the framework in which the dancer and choreographer create movement. Not every imaginable movement is possible within the constraints of human anatomy or of physical law. Movement conceived by the choreographer and implemented by the dancer is most effective when those constraints are well understood. Dancers, dance teachers, choreographers, and observers of dance are recognizing the enormous value of an understanding of these constraints. When the inherent limitations *are* deeply understood, they cease to be constraints, and instead emerge as a framework that is an integral part of the beauty of dance movement.

The aim of this book has been to help build that physical framework within which dance movement exists. We can assure you, the reader, that the physical principles are sound and do indeed apply to the human body. The challenge is to make an understanding of this framework not a mere abstraction, but *useful* in a way that contributes to an appreciation of the beauty of dance.

# Linear Mechanics and Newton's Laws

Mechanics is a study of the properties of motion of massive objects in response to forces acting on them. The description of motion itself is "kinematics," involving relationships between position, velocity, acceleration, and time. "Dynamics" involves the relationships between motion and the causes of changes in the state of motion. A deeper treatment of mechanics can be found in any of a number of college-level introductory physics textbooks.

## Kinematics

*Position* is a description of the location of a point representing a particle or some specified point in an extended object. Position can be described in one dimension (along a line such as the vertical line important in describing the characteristics of vertical jumps or lifts), two dimensions (as in defining location on a stage floor), or three dimensions (necessary for describing jumps moving around a stage area).

*Velocity* is the rate of change of position, given by the distance traveled divided by the time required, and directed from the earlier position to the later. For instance, a dancer moving 15 feet from upstage center to downstage center in three seconds has a velocity of 5 feet per second toward downstage. *Speed* is just the magnitude of velocity, with no direction specified. The speed of that dancer would be 5 feet per second.

*Acceleration* is the rate of change of velocity, given by the difference between a later velocity and an earlier velocity, divided by the time required for the change. Note that an acceleration results from a change in the magnitude of the velocity *or* from a change in its direction. If the dancer moving downstage slows to a stop in one second, the acceleration would be 5 feet per second *per second*, directed *upstage*. If the dancer moving downstage *reverses* his velocity in one second so that he is then moving upstage at 5 feet per second, and this reversal takes one second, the acceleration is 10 feet per second *per second*. Note that the speed is 5 feet per second before and after the acceleration, but the velocity has changed significantly because the direction of motion has changed. As we will see later, any change in velocity requires a force.

A special case of changing direction of velocity is motion at a constant speed in a circle. That motion is accelerated toward the center of the circle because of the constantly changing direction of velocity, even if the motion stays at a constant radius from the center.

Several useful relationships, called the "kinematic" equations, can be derived that relate the quantities that describe motion— distance, velocity, acceleration, and time. These relationships allow us to relate time of flight to height of a jump, and to calculate forces required for certain movements. The simplest of these relationships is

$$s = vt,$$

where $v$ is the average velocity during the time $t$ taken to travel the distance $s$. Acceleration and velocity are related by

$$v_2 - v_1 = at,$$

where $a$ is the average acceleration during the time $t$ it takes to change the velocity from $v_1$ to $v_2$. Other useful relationships are:

$$v_2^2 - v_1^2 = 2\,a\,s$$

and

$$s = \tfrac{1}{2}\,a\,t^2$$

From this last equation we can derive a relationship between the height of a jump and the time in the air. A body acted upon by no forces other than gravity (a "free-fall" condition) will accelerate downward at a constant acceleration, $g$, which has a numerical value of 32 feet per second per second for any mass. In the above equation, $t$ is the time during which the body is accelerating downward from its highest point, $s$ is the distance from the highest point to the ground, and $a$ is the acceleration due to gravity, $g$. Solving for $t$ produces the equation

$$t = \sqrt{\frac{2s}{g}}.$$

Recognizing that $s$ is just the height of the jump $H$, and that it takes the same length of time to slow to a stop while rising as it takes to accelerate back down to the floor, we have the equation relating the *total time in the air T* to the height of a jump:

$$T = 2\sqrt{\frac{2H}{g}}.$$

A jump one foot high will thus produce a time in the air of one-half second for *any* body.

The preceding discussions have dealt with kinematics, or relationships between the variables that describe motion. Let us turn now to *dynamics*, or analyses of motions of bodies in response to forces.

## Dynamics

Newton's three laws of motion, which he developed in the seventeenth century, form the basis of essentially all of classical dynamics. They can be stated as follows:

Newton's first law: In the absence of any interaction with the rest of the universe, a body will either remain at rest or move in a straight line with a constant velocity.

Newton's second law: If a force $F$ is applied to a body of mass $m$, the resulting acceleration $a$ is given by $a = F/m$.

Newton's third law: If body one exerts on body two a force $F_{12}$, then body two exerts a force on body one of $F_{21}$, which is equal in magnitude but opposite in direction to $F_{12}$.

Some examples of the application of these laws will be useful. Although it usually takes some force to keep an object moving, that force is necessary only to overcome unavoidable friction or drag forces that act in a direction opposing the motion. A dancer moving across a floor will move in a straight line at constant speed unless there is some external force acting to change the dancer's state of motion. That force may be another dancer or a force from the floor.

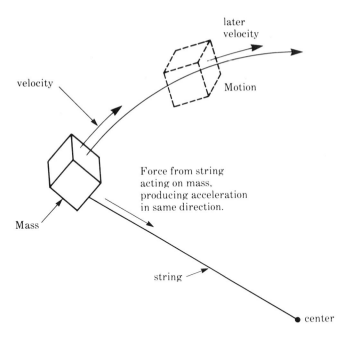

FIGURE A-1   This diagram shows the "centripetal" force towards the center of a circular path, which keeps the mass moving in its curved path.

Circular motion is motion with a constantly changing direction. Since the velocity is changing, there is an acceleration, and a force is necessary to produce that acceleration. If you whirl a ball around your head on the end of a string you must exert an inward force on the string to keep the ball moving in its curved path. A dancer moving in a circular path must have a force exerted on him by the floor similar to that of the string, again directed toward the center of the circular motion, as shown in figure A-1.

The second law relates the magnitude of the force to the resulting acceleration. A heavy person (one with large weight and mass) requires a larger force to cause a change in velocity at a certain rate than does a small person. The gravitational field of the earth produces a downward vertical force on a body. This force, called the *weight*, is proportional to the body's mass. However, although the downward force on the heavy body is greater, the inertial mass that limits the acceleration is also greater. That is, the acceleration that results from a given force is inversely proportional to the mass and thus is smaller for greater masses. So the larger mass has a greater gravitational force acting on it, but that greater force is just enough to accelerate the larger mass with the same acceleration as for a smaller mass. As a result, the downward acceleration, $g$, due to the gravitational force, is the same for all bodies and is numerically equal to 32 feet per second per second. Thus, in the absence of the force of air resistance, all objects would accelerate in free fall at the same rate, and would take the same time to fall a given distance. This result was supposedly demonstrated by Galileo in the well-known story of two objects dropped from the leaning tower of Pisa.

The third law is very important in dance, as any accelerations require forces exerted on the body, and the body is exerting equal and opposite forces on the agent of the accelerating force. That is, if a dancer wishes to accelerate toward the front of a stage, he must exert a force against the stage to the rear, and the stage will then exert the equal and opposite forward accelerating force on the dancer. A common question among beginning students of physics is "How can there be any acceleration of a body if any force is balanced by an equal and opposite force?" The answer is that those equal and opposite forces are acting on different things—the floor and the dancer. There is still an unbalanced force *on the dancer's body*, causing *it* to accelerate.

What forces are exerted on a person standing at rest on a floor? Since the body is not accelerating, the sum of all forces acting on the body must be zero. Earth's gravity exerts a downward force that effectively acts at the center of gravity of the body, and the floor exerts a vertical upward force on the body through the feet. The body exerts an accompanying downward force on the floor.

Now consider the forces acting on the part of the body above the waist. The gravitation of the earth exerts a force downward on the upper body that is equal to the weight of that portion of the body (perhaps half of the total body weight). That force is balanced by an upward force exerted by the lower body on the upper body. There are no other forces acting on the upper body as a whole, so that compressive force must exist in the body at the waist, no matter how one is "placed," "pulled up," or whatever. In fact, since the internal organs of the body can support little compressive force, most of that force is effectively borne by the spine. The compressive force in the spine is a maximum at the base of the spine, because there is more of the body weight to be supported above that point than above a higher point. Of course, at the feet, the entire body's weight must be supported by a compressive force exerted on what may be a small area of the foot on *demi-pointe* or *pointe*.

Suppose now that a partner is lifting a dancer by the waist. If the dancer is suspended motionless aloft, the lifting force exerted by the partner must equal the dancer's weight. But for the lifted person, that force is no longer a compressive force at the feet. The lower half of the body is now suspended with extension or stretching forces, while the upper body remains under compression, as when standing on the floor. A lift by the armpits results in most of the body experiencing extension forces, with only the upper spine and neck supporting compressive forces. These changes in the distribution of compressive and extension forces challenge the lifted dancer to maintain body placement and line that are aesthetically pleasing.

One of the most valuable concepts in the application of physical principles of dance involves linear and rotational momentum. (The latter will be discussed in appendix B.) Momentum can be thought of as a quantity of motion, involving both the mass of a body and its velocity. The magnitude of linear momentum is just the product of mass and velocity, and its direction is the direction of the velocity. It can be shown that momentum is a conserved quantity—that is, the momentum of a system does not change if there are no total forces acting on it, even if there are interactions or changes within the system. Suppose one person moving horizontally collides with another. If friction is ignored, the total momentum of the two after the collision will equal the total momentum of the two before, which will be just the momentum of the first person if the second was initially at rest. An example of this phenomenon occurs with a partnered running catch. If a woman has a certain linear momentum while running to her standing partner, then jumps to be caught by him, their combined momentum just after the catch will equal her momentum before. The "catcher" then can be seen to decelerate their combined mass by exerting a force against the floor to slow their forward motion.

A single body may also be considered as a "system" composed of many parts. If the body is at rest with no outside forces acting on it, and one part is displaced to one side, the rest of the body will recoil in the opposite direction, maintaining a zero total momentum of the system.

# *Rotational Mechanics*

A set of laws and kinematic equations may be developed for rotational motion quite analogous to those described for linear motion in appendix A. If $A$ is a rotational displacement (or change in rotational orientation) in degrees of arc, $\omega$ (the Greek lowercase "omega") is rotational velocity (or rate of turn, or turning speed) in degrees per second, $\alpha$ (Greek "alpha") is rotational acceleration or the rate at which the turning speed changes, and $t$ is time, then

$$A = \omega t,$$

$$\omega_2 - \omega_1 = \alpha t,$$

$$\omega_2^2 - \omega_1^2 = 2 \alpha A, \text{ and}$$

$$A = \tfrac{1}{2} \alpha t^2.$$

Recall the dancer in appendix A who was moving downstage at a velocity of 5 feet per second. A rotational analogue would be a dancer turning at a rate of, let's say, one revolution (a 360° turn) every two seconds, for a rotational velocity of 180° per second. If two seconds later she is rotating at a rate of a full revolution every second, or 360° per second, the rotational acceleration would be the difference in those rotational velocities divided by two seconds, the time interval during which the rotational velocity changed, or 90° per second per second. The other two equations follow by analogy with their linear counterparts in the same way.

The rotational analogue of Newton's laws of linear motion may be expressed by substituting variables appropriate for the

TABLE B-1    Analogous linear and rotational quantities for kinematics and dynamics.

| Quantity | Linear | Rotational |
|---|---|---|
| Time | $t$ | $t$ |
| Position | $s$ | $A$ |
| Velocity | $v$ | $\omega$ |
| Acceleration | $a$ | $\alpha$ |
| Cause of change in motion | Force ($F$) | Torque ($T$) |
| Inertia | Mass ($m$) | Rotational Inertia ($I$) |
| Momentum | $p$ | $L$ |

description of rotational motion for the corresponding linear quantities, giving rise to a system of equations for rotational dynamics. In this case position, velocity, and acceleration are replaced by their rotational counterparts, force is replaced by "torque," which may be thought of as a turning force, and mass is replaced by "rotational inertia," which is a measure of a body's inertial resistance to a change in rotational motion. (See table B-1.)

A torque arises from a force acting on a body along a line displaced from its center of gravity. For convenience we will consider torques that produce no linear acceleration; in that case a torque is produced by a force "couple," which is two equal and opposite forces acting on a body, for which the lines of action of the forces are not coincident, but are parallel with some distance $d$ between them, as in the diagram in figure B-1. The magnitude of the torque is given by the product of the force and the separation distance $d$, called the "moment arm."

One example of a force couple is the opposite forces exerted by the two separated feet when a dancer begins a *pirouette*. Another is the opposite tangential forces exerted by the two hands of a partner when initiating the supported *fouetté pirouette* described in chapter 9. If the right hand pulls back and the left hand pushes forward at the waist of the partnered dancer, she will be given a rotational acceleration toward the right, or clockwise as viewed from above.

The rotational inertia depends on the mass of a body and its distribution relative to the axis of rotation. A body of given mass will have a larger rotational inertia if the mass is far from the axis of rotation than if it is close. An *arabesque* or *à la seconde* position has a larger rotational inertia than a *retiré* or *passé* position.

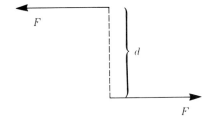

FIGURE B-1    A force couple. The two forces have equal magnitudes "F."

The rotational analogue of Newton's second law can be simply stated:

$$T = F\,d = I\,\alpha$$

where $T$ is the torque whose magnitude is given by the product of the force and the separation distance for a force couple, $I$ is the rotational inertia, and $\alpha$ is the rotational acceleration. Clearly, if the torque is zero there is no rotational acceleration, and the rotational velocity is constant (perhaps zero). If there *is* a torque, its magnitude is large if either the force is large or the separation between the parallel lines of action of the forces is large. For instance, a *pirouette* from fifth position, for which the separation of the forces is small, is more difficult to initiate than a *pirouette* from fourth position with the feet separated. For a given torque, the rotational velocity will increase rapidly if $I$ is small, which will be true if the body's mass is compacted close to the axis of rotation. Chapter 9 deals with torques and force couples as they apply to the initiation of supported *pirouettes*.

A powerful concept for dance analysis involves rotational momentum. Analogous to linear momentum, rotational momentum $L$ is given by the product of the rotational inertia $I$ and rotational velocity. Thus

$$L = I\,\omega$$

If there are no torques on a body, rotational momentum is a conserved quantity, meaning that $L$ is a constant. But now, unlike the case of linear momentum in which the mass is constant, both the rotational inertia and the rotational velocity can change. This fact has broad implications. For instance, even if there are no torques to change a dancer's rotational momentum around a vertical axis, the rotational velocity can still be changed by causing a change in the distribution of mass relative to the axis of rotation. A spinning ice skater increases the rate of turn by bringing arms and legs closer to the axis. Or a dancer doing a *grande pirouette* speeds up noticeably when the arms and legs are brought from an extended position into a normal *pirouette* position. In linear motion, since it is impossible to change one's mass or weight suddenly, the linear velocity cannot be changed without some force being exerted on the body to change its linear momentum.

If there *is* a torque, there will generally be a rotational acceleration. But because both the rotational inertia and the rotational

FIGURE B-2   The rotational inertia depends on the body configuration; it is greater when the
body is extended than when it
is close to the axis of rotation.

velocity can change, the dynamic equation relating torque to change in rotational motion is actually a little more subtle than that given earlier. The more general relationship is that *the torque is equal to the rate of change of rotational momentum*. In the special case of constant rotational inertia, this relationship reduces to

$$T = I\alpha$$

as stated before. But now one can see that, for a given torque, the rotational acceleration will be small if $I$ is large. This is desirable if one wants to acquire a significant rotational momentum without accelerating too rapidly away from the initial position from which the accelerating torque is exerted. After the rotational momentum is acquired, the rotational inertia can be decreased, thus allowing the rotational velocity to increase. This process is particularly noticeable in a *pirouette en dedans* with *dégagé à la seconde*, in which the back push-off foot swings out while the body turns very little, then moves in to *pirouette* position as the body turns more rapidly.

Note that the "rotations" described here may involve not only rotations of the body as a whole, but of its individual parts. For instance, when the legs move in a scissorlike motion back and forth ("beats" in dance), they are actually rotating around an axis at the hip joint. The beats of the legs moving apart and then back together are rotational oscillations, requiring rotational accelerations outward and then inward. For these accelerations, muscles around the hip joint exert forces along lines displaced from the center of rotation in the joint, producing the required torques.

# *Anatomical Data for a Dancer*

Quantifying body segment lengths and masses for dancers is no easy task. Lengths of thighs, forearms, and other body parts can be measured directly, but determining their masses and quantifying their shapes is far more challenging. Some information that has been used for many years involved the weighing of dismembered cadavers. Other techniques have been less precise, but more applicable to typical participants in sports and dance.

More than twenty years ago Stanley Plagenhoef[1-3] summarized the work of several investigators who determined, by measurement or modeling, body segment masses and lengths. The data include averages for six female college-age gymnasts (presumed to be more representative of dancers than the general female population), and for thirty-five college-age men. This information is summarized in table C-1.

More recent data, using modern techniques of measurement, have been reported by Zatsiorsky, et al. (1990),[4] and evaluated and interpreted by Paolo de Leva from the Instituto Superiore di Educazione Fisica di Roma, Italy, and Indiana University Kinesiology Department (Bloomington). The test group of females for this latter data comprised nine college athletes in track-and-field and diving. The data include not only masses and lengths of body segments, but carefully defined end points for the segments and locations of their centers of gravity. The test group, however, is not as applicable to the dance population, as the average of the females' total height was about 4 percent greater than that used in these appendixes for a slender female dancer, but with a body weight 32 percent greater. Data for male athletes differed only slightly from that reported by Plagenhoef. So data summarized in *The Physics of Dance* ten years ago still seem to be the most viable for these purposes.

TABLE C-1   Weights (in percentage of total body weight) and lengths (in percentage of total body height) of body segments for six female college-age gymnasts and 35 college-age men, after Plagenhoef.

| Body Segment | Men | | Women | |
|---|---|---|---|---|
| | Weight | Length | Weight | Length |
| Trunk | 48.3 | 30.0 | 50.8 | 30.0 |
| Head | 7.1 | | 9.4 | |
| Thigh | 10.5 | 23.2 | 8.3 | 24.7 |
| Shank | 4.5 | 24.7 | 5.5 | 25.6 |
| Foot | 1.5 | | 1.2 | |
| Upper arm | 3.3 | 17.2 | 2.7 | 19.3 |
| Forearm | 1.9 | 15.7 | 1.6 | 16.6 |
| Hand | 0.6 | | 0.5 | |

## Notes

1. S. Plagenhoef, *Patterns of Human Motion* (Englewood Cliffs, NJ: Prentice-Hall, 1971), chapter 3.
2. Plagenhoef, after W. T. Dempster, "Space Requirements of the Seated Operator," *WADC Technical Report* (1955): 55-159.
3. Plagenhoef, after K. Kjeldsen, "Body Segment Weights of College Women" (Master's thesis, University of Massachusetts, 1969).
4. V. M. Zatsiorsky, V. N. Seluyanov, and L. G. Chugunova, "Methods of Determining Mass-inertial Characteristics of Human Body Segments," in G. G. Chernyi, and S. A. Regirer, Eds., *Contemporary Problems of Biomechanics* (Boca Raton, MA: CRC Press, 1990), 272-291.

# Rotational Inertia for Some Body Configurations

There are two ways the rotational inertia is important in analyzing the dynamics of rotational motion. First, for a given torque, the rotational inertia determines the change of rotational momentum occurring in a particular time interval. Second, if the torque is zero (or approximately zero), rotational velocity is related to the rotational inertia, which can be changed by varying the body configuration. That is, since the rotational momentum is a constant when the torque is zero, a change in body position that causes the rotational inertia to double will decrease the rotational velocity by one-half. (See appendix B for a more complete discussion of rotational motion.)

Several analyses require knowing the rotational inertia of the body or parts of the body in various positions and around various axes. Before making those calculations, let us consider some simple geometrical shapes. A point mass of mass $M$ revolving on the end of a string a distance $R$ from the center of rotation will have a rotational inertia $I = MR^2$. Geometrical shapes in which the mass is distributed through some volume of the object may be treated as a collection of point masses, each having some small mass and an associated distance from the rotation axis. Table D-1 gives some representative moments of inertia for simple geometrical shapes.

TABLE D-1   Rotational inertia values for some simple geometrical shapes.

| Shape | Axis | Rotational Inertia |
|---|---|---|
| | Middle | $\frac{1}{12} M L^2$ |
| Rod, length $L$ | One end | $\frac{1}{3} M L^2$ |
| | Distance $D$ beyond one end | $M \left\{ \frac{1}{12} L^2 + (D + \frac{1}{2} L)^2 \right\}$ |
| Cylinder, radius $R$, length $L$ | Center axis | $\frac{1}{2} M R^2$ |
| | Parallel edge | $\frac{3}{2} M R^2$ |
| Sphere, radius $R$ | Center | $\frac{2}{5} M R^2$ |
| Circular ring, radius $R$ | Edge, perpendicular to plane | $2 M R^2$ |

FIGURE D-1   Different shapes of objects for which values of rotational inertia are calculated for later use.

One rotational inertia we will need is that of a rigid leg oscillating around a horizontal axis through the hip joint. A rough calculation will give a good idea of the magnitude of this rotational inertia for a male of height $6'\frac{1}{2}''$ (about 1.84 m) and weight 159 lbs (72 kg). (These figures roughly fit Sean Lavery, the model for the movements described in chapter 6.) The total rotational

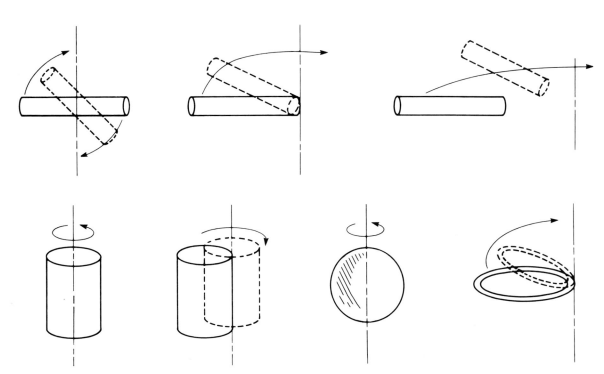

*Rotational Inertia for Some Body Configurations*

inertia of the leg will be made up of contributions from the thigh, shank, and foot. Data from appendix C will be used, along with equations for moments of inertia of uniform masses. The thigh is assumed to be a uniform rod oscillating around one end. The shank is a uniform rod oscillating around an axis $l_1 + \frac{1}{2} l_2$ from its center of gravity. We will assume the foot to be a point mass a distance $l_1 + l_2$ from the axis through the hip. (The subscripts 1, 2, and 3 refer to the thigh, shank, and foot, respectively.) The total rotational inertia is then

$$ I = \tfrac{1}{3} m_1 l_1^2 + m_2 \left[ \tfrac{1}{12} l_2^2 + \left( l_1 + \tfrac{1}{2} l_2 \right)^2 \right] + m_3 \left( l_1 + l_2 \right)^2. $$

Using the data for Sean, the tall dancer, and Shorty of chapter 6 (Sean is 15 percent larger than Shorty in all linear dimensions), the magnitudes of moments of inertia for the oscillating leg are

$$ I = 2.75 \text{ kg-m}^2 \text{ for Sean, and} $$
$$ I = 1.37 \text{ kg-m}^2 \text{ for Shorty.} $$

Now consider another important body configuration—the normal *pirouette* position. This will be idealized as a vertical body with the gesture leg in *retiré* (foot at the opposite knee), and the arms making a horizontal circle in front of the body. These calculations will be somewhat crude, but it is important to recognize two aspects of this analysis. First, bodies differ significantly, so accuracy in the calculations is not useful. Second, the purpose here will be to demonstrate some relative magnitudes of moments of inertia, which lead to interesting characteristics of the motions involved, rather than to develop accurate quantitative analyses. Let us take as our example a female of height 1.6 m (5′ 3″) and mass 44 kg (97 lbs). Assume the head and trunk form a uniform cylinder of effective radius 12 cm, rotating around its vertical axis of symmetry along with the supporting leg, having an effective average radius of 4 cm. These estimates of radius are crude, and take into account the fact that mass far from the axis is weighted more heavily than mass close to the axis. The hips, for instance, contribute a significant fraction of the rotational inertia of the rotating body, because they are generally larger in women than other parts of the body.

Adding the different contributions to the total rotational inertia, the value for this symmetric part of the body is:

$$ I_1 = \tfrac{1}{2} m r^2 = 0.20 \text{ kg-m}^2, $$

using the data of appendix C and our sample female. The gesture leg forms an equilateral triangle to the side of the axis of rotation. Its contribution to the total $I$ is

$$I_2 = \tfrac{1}{3} (m_1 + m_2) (l \cos 30°)^2 = 0.25 \text{ kg-m}^2,$$

where $m_1$ and $m_2$ are the masses of the thigh and shank, respectively. The arms form a circle of radius about 20 cm, with the axis through one edge. Their contribution to the total rotational inertia is

$$I_3 = 2\, m_a\, r^2 = 0.17 \text{ kg-m}^2,$$

where $m_a$ is the total mass of the arms. The total rotational inertia of a body rotating in *pirouette* position is thus

$$I = 0.62 \text{ kg-m}^2.$$

Now, for the purpose of analyzing the *fouetté* turn, consider the rotational inertia of the gesture leg alone as it is extended horizontally to the front and rotates to the side. This is effectively the same physical rotation as the oscillating leg analyzed earlier. The total $I$ is

$$I_l = 2.55 \text{ kg-m}^2.$$

In appendix I a solo *fouetté* turn is analyzed numerically; in appendix J a supported *fouetté* turn, or "whip turn," is analyzed.

APPENDIX *E*

# Acceleration away from Balance

Imagine the body as an idealized "stick" of length $L$ somewhat heavier at the upper end than the lower. This stick can be balanced vertically on the floor. If it is displaced from the vertical by a small initial angle $\theta_0$ it will start toppling, and the angle $\theta$ will increase at an accelerating rate.

The force of gravity acts on the center of gravity, and thus exerts a torque around the point of support whenever the stick is displaced from the vertical. (See figure E-1.) The equation relating the rotational acceleration $\alpha$ away from the vertical and the torque $T$ due to gravity is

$$T = m \, g \, R_c \sin \theta = I \, \alpha = m \, R_g^2 \alpha$$

where $m$ is the mass of the body, $g$ is the acceleration due to gravity, $R_c$ is the distance from the point of support to the center of gravity, $I$ is the rotational inertia of the body toppling around an axis through the point of support, $R_g$ is the radius of gyration (defined as $\sqrt{I/m}$), and $\alpha$ is the toppling rotational acceleration. If the angle is small, $\sin \theta$ may be replaced by $\theta$ with very little error. There results a simple differential equation which has as a solution, taking into account the initial conditions,

$$\theta = \theta_0 \cosh \left[ \sqrt{g \, R_c / R_g^2} \, \right] t$$

where $\cosh K t$ represents a hyperbolic cosine function of time $t$ with constant coefficient $K$, where $K$ has the value $\sqrt{g \, R_c / R_g^2}$.

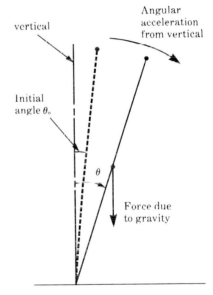

FIGURE E-1   The toppling of a vertical rod.

For a uniform stick of length 5′ 10″ (or 1.78 m), the center of mass would be at the midpoint, so $R_c = 0.89$ m; $R_g$ would be 1.03 m. Assuming the body is more massive at the upper end, let us increase each of these quantities arbitrarily by 15 percent. Thus $R_c = 1.02$ m and $R_g = 1.18$ m, and the coefficient of $t$ in the above equation has the numerical value 2.7 / s.

Note that this coefficient is greater for a small person, so that the acceleration away from vertical is, as one would expect, more rapid than for a larger person.

Table E-1 shows the angle of displacement from the vertical in degrees as it varies with time for a few initial angles of displacement, for a 5′ 10″ dancer and one 15 percent smaller (just under 5′). Note how rapidly the angle increases, doubling about every quarter second after the early acceleration from vertical. Even for relatively small initial angles, the toppling is very rapid after a time of only a second or so. The challenge to dancers is for them to assure that they are initially as close as possible to the balance condition, and that they carry out the appropriate motions to adjust balance very quickly, before the departure from vertical is too large to correct.

TABLE E-1   Increase of angle of displacement from the vertical for tall and short toppling dancers, for different initial angles of displacement.

| Height | Time (seconds) | Angle from Vertical (degrees) | | | |
|---|---|---|---|---|---|
| | start | 0.5 | 1.0 | 2.0 | 4.0 |
| | 0.5 | 1.0 | 2.1 | 4.1 | 8.2 |
| 5′10″ | 1.0 | 3.7 | 7.5 | 15 | 30 |
| | 1.5 | 14 | 29 | 57 | >60 |
| | 2.0 | 55 | >60 | >60 | >60 |
| | start | 0.5 | 1.0 | 2.0 | 4.0 |
| | 0.5 | 1.1 | 2.3 | 4.5 | 9.0 |
| 5′ | 1.0 | 4.6 | 9.1 | 18 | 36 |
| | 1.5 | 20 | 39 | >60 | >60 |
| | 2.0 | >60 | >60 | >60 | >60 |

*Acceleration away from Balance*

# *Off-Balance* Pirouettes

Suppose a dancer is off balance while performing a *pirouette*. What action is necessary in order for the dancer to regain balance?

The choice of the appropriate technique of analysis depends on the magnitude of spinning rotational momentum. If this $L$ is not very large, then the effects of rotation can be ignored, and the process of restoring balance can be analyzed as if the dancer were not rotating but just poised above the supporting point at the floor. If the spinning rotational momentum *is* large, then the motion and its analysis are more complicated. The turning dancer would have to be treated like a spinning top (or gyroscope), with the possibility of precession of the rotation axis (the circling of the axis of a top around the vertical when it is off balance).

In order to make a judgment about the magnitude of the spinning rotational momentum, that $L$ must be compared with the toppling rotational momentum produced by the torque due to gravity acting on the unbalanced body. This torque is given in appendix E as

$$T = m \, g \, R_c \sin \theta$$

where $m$ is the mass of the body, $g$ is the acceleration due to gravity, $R_c$ is the height to the center of gravity, and $\theta$ is the angle of lean of the body from the vertical. In appendix B it was pointed out that torque equals the rate of change of rotational momentum, so that a change in rotational momentum occurring in a time $\Delta t$ is given by

$$\Delta L = (m\ g\ R_c \sin \theta )\ \Delta t$$

If the body spins through many revolutions while the $\Delta L$ causes a small change in direction of the almost-vertical spinning $L$ associated with the spinning, then precession results, and the dancer's balance is essentially maintained without adjustments having to be made.

Let us estimate some numerical values of the quantities involved. Assume a female dancer of mass 50 kg (110 lbs), height 1.7 m (5′ 7″), rotating in normal *pirouette* position at a rotational velocity of two revolutions per second, or 12.6 rad/s. As shown in appendix D, her rotational inertia will be about 0.7 kg-m$^2$. Her rotational momentum of spin will then be

$$L = I\omega = (0.7)\ (12.6) = 8.8\ kg\text{-}m^2/s.$$

Now consider the toppling. The dancer's center of gravity is about 1.0 m above the floor. Suppose the angle of displacement from the vertical is 2°. (Ignoring the rotating motion, that angle would increase to about 4° after $\frac{1}{2}$ second.) The torque is then 17 kg-m$^2$/s$^2$, giving rise to a change of rotational momentum of 8.5 kg-m$^2$/s in the half-second it takes to complete one revolution of the *pirouette*.

It appears that the condition for precession mentioned earlier is *not* met; the change in rotational momentum occurring while the body is turning through many revolutions is *not small* compared to the spin rotational momentum, and the rotation can be ignored. Of course, if the angle of displacement is significantly smaller than 2°, or if the turn rate is greater, the rotation *would* be important. In that case, the rotation would actually *help* a dancer maintain balance, for the same reason a top topples more slowly when spinning than when not spinning. But in most cases the adjustments in balance must be made as if the rotational momentum of rotation could be ignored.

APPENDIX *G*

# Arabesque *Turn Analysis*

One potential problem in performing an *arabesque* turn is the "drooping leg syndrome." The gesture leg, which is supposed to be extended roughly horizontally to the rear, tends to descend during the turn because of the downward pull of gravity. The rotational inertia of the rotating body decreases as the leg's mass is brought down and therefore closer to the axis of rotation, allowing the rotational velocity to increase. The more rapid rotation produces an increase in the centrifugal force tending to throw the gesture leg back out to the rear, giving rise to an up-and-down oscillation of the leg.

This problem was described in chapter 4, and the result of a detailed analysis was mentioned indicating that the period of oscillation of the leg can be close to the period of rotation, making the problem particularly insidious. The more detailed analysis will now be described.

The body is assumed to consist of three main body parts, as shown in the diagram of figure G-1. The effect of the arms in contributing to the rotational inertia will be ignored because they are so light, and the contribution of the supporting leg will be ignored because its mass is concentrated so close to the axis of rotation. The axis of rotation will be assumed to lie in a vertical line along the edge of the cylindrical torso and head. We will assume a female of height 5′ 3″ (1.60 m), weight 97 lbs (44 kg), and effective radius of the torso 12 cm. The other masses and body segment lengths are taken from appendix C.

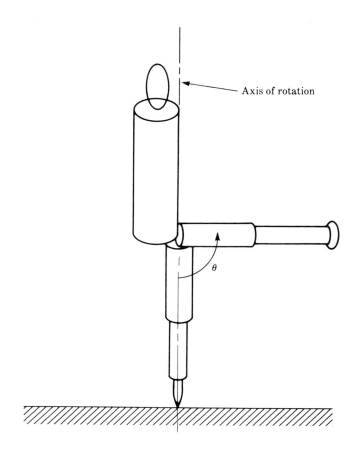

Axis of rotation

The total rotational inertia of a cylinder rotating around an axis along its edge is

$$I_b = 3/2 \, M_b \, r^2 = 0.66 \text{ kg-m}^2.$$

The rotational inertia of the gesture leg making an angle $\theta$ with the vertical is

$$I_l = I_0 \sin^2 \theta,$$

where $I_0 = 1.44$ kg-m$^2$, from a calculation similar to that found in appendix D.

The effect of the centrifugal force on the leg can be treated as a torque around a horizontal axis through the hip, tending to increase the angle $\theta$. This torque is proportional to the square of the rotational velocity $\omega$, and is given numerically (after integrating over the length of the leg and substituting assumed masses and lengths) as

$$T_l = (144 \text{ kg-m}^2) \, \omega^2 \sin \theta \cos \theta.$$

The torque tending to decrease $\theta$ (lower the leg) is due to gravity acting on the center of gravity of the leg, and is found to be

$$T_2 = (\ 25.5\ \text{kg-m}^2/\text{s}^2\ )\ \sin \theta.$$

The total torque on the leg tending to increase its angle with the vertical is thus, in standard meter-kilogram-second units,

$$T = 144\ \omega^2\ \sin \theta \cos \theta - 25.5 \sin \theta$$

The rotational momentum of the rotating body will be assumed constant (no accelerating or retarding torques between the supporting foot and the floor). What is this rotational momentum? Let us choose a rotation rate of 0.8 revolutions per second, with the leg at the equilibrium angle for that rotation rate, such that the dancer is exerting no torque in the hip to support the leg. (This is artificial, since most dancers *will* exert a torque to help support the leg. That torque will be taken into account later as a perturbing factor in the simpler analysis.)

The equilibrium angle can be found by setting the total torque in the above equation to zero and finding the $\theta$ that corresponds to the assumed value of $\omega$. The result is $\theta_o = 45°$. Now, with that $\theta$ the total rotational inertia can be found from the first equation, and the rotational momentum is

$$L = 6.95\ \text{kg-m}^2/\text{s}.$$

If this rotational momentum is a constant even when the angle $\theta$ and the rotation rate change, we can use that fact to eliminate $\omega$ from the equation for total torque. The rotational velocity is given by

$$\omega = L / I = \frac{6.95}{I_h + I_0 \sin^2 \theta} = \frac{4.84}{0.46 + \sin^2 \theta}.$$

Now we can construct an expression for the torque tending to change the leg angle $\theta$ in terms of just one variable, $\theta$. Since torque is the product of the rotational inertia of the leg around the horizontal hip axis and the rotational acceleration $\alpha$ of the leg around that axis, we have a final expression

$$1.44\ \alpha = 1.44 \left[\frac{4.84}{0.46 + \sin^2 \theta}\right]^2 \sin \theta \cos \theta - 25.5 \sin \theta.$$

This is a nontrivial differential equation, which can be solved by assuming the change of $\theta$ from $\theta_o$ is small. The numerical result of this solution is that the frequency of oscillation is about 1.1 cycles per second. This frequency is close enough to the turn rate of 0.8 revolutions per second that, with the significant uncertainties in the analysis, the two may be equal, giving rise to a "resonance" in which the leg undergoes one up-down-up oscillation while the body turns one complete turn. There is undoubtedly a mental reinforcement for an oscillation that involves a slowing of the body's rotation each time the dancer is facing the side, with the *arabesque* line facing the audience. This reinforcement would be particularly strong if the head is also spotting to that direction once each revolution.

Now suppose the cavalier assumption about the lack of torque from the hip is reconsidered. Suppose the hip exerts a constant lifting torque such that the equilibrium angle of the leg is increased to 75° from the vertical. The torque necessary to accomplish that more nearly horizontal *arabesque* position can be calculated, and has a numerical value of

$$T_H = 15.6 \text{ kg-m}^2/\text{s}^2 \ .$$

The total constant rotational momentum is greater in this case, since the leg is extended farther from the axis of rotation. The relationship between the rotational acceleration of the leg around the hip joint and the angle $\theta$ must take into account the additional hip torque. A solution of the revised equation produces the result that the oscillation frequency is 0.9 cycles per second, a bit slower than for oscillations around the lower angle of 45°. In fact, this oscillation frequency is even closer to the frequency of rotation, implying an even closer coupling between the rotation and the oscillating leg.

Again, the result is important in that the natural tendency to slow the turn, or pause, after each revolution is enhanced by the "drooping leg syndrome," in which the leg is high and the rotation slow, then the leg descends, speeding the turn, then rises again after about one revolution to slow the turn when the body again is facing the original direction. The fact that the movement is performed without the culprit leg in sight of the dancer makes it difficult to correct this fault which has such a negative effect on the aesthetic line of the *arabesque* position during the turn.

# *Quantitative Analysis of the* Grande Pirouette

The *grande pirouette* is a turn on one supporting leg with the gesture leg extended horizontally to the side (second position *en l'air*). A detailed analysis is quite involved, even when several simplifying assumptions are made. The results of the analysis will be outlined here.

Assume the body can be represented by two legs, each of mass $m$ and length $l$ (and negligible thickness), plus the remainder of the body, of mass $M$, effective length $L$, symmetric around the longitudinal axis. The legs consist of a thigh of length $\frac{1}{2} l$ and mass $\frac{2}{3} m$, and a shank and foot of length $\frac{1}{2} l$ and mass $\frac{1}{3} m$. (These assumptions are within a few percent of data on human bodies given by Plagenhoef and described in appendix C.) Leg number 1, the supporting leg, makes an angle $\theta$ with the vertical; leg number 2, the gesture leg, is horizontal; the remainder of the body is effectively vertical. (See figure H-1.)

Now the question is whether there is a difference in the angle $\theta$ for static equilibrium and for the case where the body is rotating about the vertical axis.

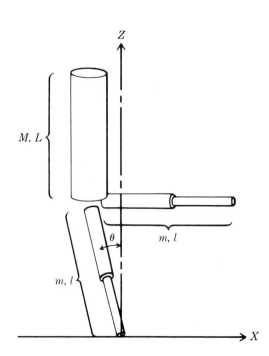

FIGURE H-1   Idealized body
model for the *grande pirouette*
analysis.

## Static Equilibrium

The condition for static equilibrium is that the torques about the
supporting point (supporting foot on the floor) must add to
zero. These torques are due to gravity acting downward on the
center of gravity of each of the body segments. Let us first find
the position of the center of gravity for each of the three segments in the idealized model of the body. Simple calculations
show that the center of gravity of the idealized leg is $\frac{7}{12}$ of the
total leg length from the foot end, or $\frac{5}{12}$ of the leg length from the
hip. The center of gravity of the remainder of the body will be
assumed to be in the center of the cylinder, since only its horizontal position is important for the analysis.

The total torque acting in a clockwise direction around the
supporting foot is now given by

$$T = - m\,g\,l\,(\tfrac{7}{12} \sin \theta\,) - M\,g\,l \sin \theta + m\,g\,l\,(\tfrac{5}{12} - \sin \theta\,)$$

## Dynamic Equilibrium

Assume the axis of rotation is vertical. For an object that is
symmetric around the vertical axis, that axis would be a "principal axis," and the rotational momentum could also be consid-

ered to have only a vertical component. But since the body in *grande pirouette* position is clearly not symmetric, the vector representing the rotational momentum will not be vertical. (In physics terms, the inertia tensor relating rotational velocity to rotational momentum will have nonzero off-diagonal elements.)

Since the rotational momentum is not vertical, it must precess around the vertical axis as the body rotates, forming a cone with the apex at the supporting point. But the rotational momentum can change only if there is a torque acting on the body. Since the only source of torque for a freely rotating body is gravitational force, we conclude that the condition derived for static balance must not be met, so that in fact there *is* a net torque just sufficient to produce the rate of change of rotational momentum giving rise to the precession.

In order to find the nonvertical component of the rotational momentum, the reader familiar with a more advanced level of physics will recognize that it is necessary to find the elements of the inertia tensor for each of the rotating body segments. It can be shown that the magnitude of torque needed is

$$T' = \omega^2 I_{xz},$$

where $I_{xz}$ is the $xz$ element of the inertia tensor. That torque is then equated to the torque equation used for static equilibrium recognizing now that that torque will not be zero, and the angle will not be 4.4°. The result of the calculation is that the angle is in fact about 3.5° for a rotation rate of one revolution per second. The effect will, of course, be stronger for a faster turn.

Thus when the body is rotating, a small correction must be made in the angle the supporting leg makes with the vertical, shifting the body toward the extended gesture leg. That is, the total body center of gravity must be displaced slightly to the right of the vertical axis through the supporting point in figure H–1. As the turn slows, the effect diminishes, and the center of gravity must be shifted back toward the vertical line through the supporting foot.

# *Quantitative Analysis of the* Fouetté *Turn*

The *fouetté* turn is described in chapter 4. The rotational inertia values necessary for analyzing this movement quantitatively were calculated in appendix D for a female dancer of height 1.6 m (5′ 3″) and mass 44 kg (97 lbs).

Assume the torque between the supporting foot and the floor is zero, so the body will coast in its rotating motion with constant rotational momentum. The mechanical process in the *fouetté* turn involves a transfer of rotational momentum between the whole rotating body during the turn and the gesture leg alone when the rest of the body is temporarily stationary *en face*. This constant rotational momentum can be expressed as

$$L = I_b \, \omega_b = I_l \, \omega_l$$

where $I_b$ and $\omega_b$ are the rotational inertia and rotational velocity of the whole body in *pirouette* position, and $I_l$ and $\omega_l$ *are those quantities for the extended leg alone.* If $\omega_b$ is about 12.6 rad/sec (2.0 revolutions per second in the *pirouette*), then, using the rotational inertia from appendix D,

$$L = (0.62) \, (12.6) = (2.55) \, (\omega_l)$$

$$\omega_l = 3.05 \text{ rad/sec} = 0.49 \text{ rev/s}.$$

Thus the leg alone will rotate around the vertical body axis at a rate of about a half revolution per second, which means that the quarter revolution needed to move the leg from front to side will occupy about a half-second.

Given the approximations used in the model for this *fouetté* turn, the time required to complete each turn ($\frac{1}{2}$ second at a 2 revolutions-per-second rate) is equal to the time during which the body is stationary while the gesture leg rotates through its quarter turn from front to side.

# *Quantitative Analysis of the Supported* Fouetté *Turn*

The supported *fouetté* turn is discussed in chapter 9, and shown in the photographs in figure 9-4. This is a movement in which, for a turn to the right, the woman starts facing the audience *en pointe* on her left supporting leg, with her right leg extended a little to the left of directly in front of her. Her partner is behind her, hands on her waist, prepared to exert a forward force with his left hand and a backward force with his right in order to initiate the turn. When he starts to exert those forces, rather than allow herself to be turned immediately, she rotates her right leg from front to side, thereby absorbing the rotational momentum developed by her partner's forces (torque) on her. After the right leg reaches the side, she brings it in to the *passé* position, thus transferring the rotational momentum gained by the leg to the body as a whole. She then rotates as in a normal *pirouette*.

What is gained by performing the supported *pirouette* in this way? Why doesn't she just allow her body to start rotating *as* her partner exerts the forces with his hands at her waist? Some quantitative calculations will demonstrate the benefit of the supported *fouetté* by allowing for a comparison of the magnitudes of rotational velocity resulting from the two techniques.

We will draw on the results derived in appendixes D and I for the magnitudes of rotational inertia values for a female ballet dancer's body. For the dancer of height 5′ 3″ weighing 97 pounds, the rotational inertia for the extended leg alone is $I_l = 2.55$ kg-m$^2$, and for the body as a whole in *pirouette* position (right leg to the side, foot at left knee) is $I_b = 0.62$ kg-m$^2$.

Let us first consider that the partner rotates the woman as she remains in a constant *pirouette* position. Suppose the partner exerts a constant torque sufficient to produce a final rotational velocity of 1.0 revolution per second, but that he can exert that torque only through the first 45° of rotation around the vertical axis from the initial position. Using the rotational kinematic equations from appendix B, the time during which he exerts the torque is then 0.25 seconds, and the magnitude of the torque, given by

$$T = I_b \, \omega \, / \, \Delta t \, .$$

is 15.6 kg-m$^2$/s$^2$, in metric units.

Now suppose that the man exerts the same torque on the woman's waist, but she starts with the right leg extended horizontally to the front and rotates it around to the side, through an angle of 90° around the vertical axis, as the torque is exerted. Since the leg is the only part of the body rotating, the new final rotational momentum is given by

$$L = I_l \, \omega_l = T \, \Delta t = T \, [ \, \pi \, / \, \omega_l \, ].$$

But when the final rotational momentum of the rotating leg is transferred to the body as a whole,

$$I_b \, \omega_b = I_l \, \omega_l.$$

Solving these equations for the final rotational velocity of the body after the leg has returned to the *pirouette* position produces the result

$$\omega_b = 2.9 \text{ rev/s,}$$

almost three times the rate of rotation produced by the first technique! Thus, the *fouetté* technique, in which rotational momentum is stored in the rotating leg while torque is being applied, is significantly more effective in producing a substantial rotation rate when compared to the more direct technique in which the turn is started with the body in the fixed *pirouette* configuration.

Why can the woman gain three times as much rotational speed when the torque exerted by her partner is the same in both cases? The important variable is *the length of time the torque is exerted*. While the leg is rotating from front to side, the woman's partner is exerting the torque for about 0.75 second rather than for the 0.25 second in the first case.

# Glossary of Dance Terms

ADAGIO.   As in music, a slow tempo: a dance in a slow tempo. *Adagios* in ballets are often performed by partners. *Adagio* sections of dance classes are done in a slow tempo.

ALLEGRO.   Dancing that is lively and fast, in comparison to *adagio*.

ARABESQUE.   Set pose. In the most common form of *arabesque*, the dancer stands on one leg, with the other leg fully extended to the rear.

ASSEMBLÉ.   Literally, "together." A jump from one foot to two feet, ending in fifth position, with the feet "assembling," or coming together, in the air.

ATTITUDE.   A pose similar to the *arabesque*, but with the raised leg bent. An *attitude en avant* is a similar position, but with a bent leg raised to the front.

BARRE.   The horizontal bar used by dancers for support and balance in the early part of a ballet class.

BATTEMENT.   A beating movement of the legs.

CABRIOLE.   A jump in which the legs beat together while in the air. The gesture leg leaves the supporting leg in a kick to any direction; the supporting leg rises to beat against it and then returns to the floor.

CHASSÉ.   Literally, "chased." A sliding step.

COUPÉ.   A movement in which one foot "cuts" in to the ankle of the supporting leg. In recent use, the *coupé* position is a standing position with one foot at the ankle of the other leg.

Couru. Running.

Dégagé. Literally, "disengaged." A small kicking movement in place.

Demi-Fouetté. A half turn in which the gesture leg kicks to the front or back, then the body turns through an angle of 180° while leaving the gesture leg pointed in its original direction. The movement may be performed as a jump or with the supporting leg remaining on the floor.

Demi-Plié. A half bending of the knees, allowing the heels to remain on the floor.

Demi-Pointe. Standing on a foot pointed except for the toes, which are flat on the floor.

Derrière. To the rear.

Devant. In front.

Développé. Literally, "developed" or "unfolded." A gradual unfolding of the leg as it rises from the floor and is extended fully in the air. As it is raised, the foot passes the knee of the supporting leg.

En Avant. Forward.

En Dedans. Inward. Specifically, a turn toward the supporting leg.

En Dehors. Outside. Specifically, a turn away from the supporting leg.

En Face. Facing front, or toward the audience.

Entrechat. A beating step of elevation in which the dancer leaps straight into the air and crosses his feet a number of times, making a weaving motion in the air. The term *entrechat* is compounded with numerals to indicate the number of movements of the legs. Entrechat six, for instance, means six movements of the legs, or three complete crossings front and back.

Fifth Position. A standing position with the feet together and turned out (pointing to the side), heel to toe and toe to heel.

Flic-Flac. A turning movement, generally at the barre, in which the working foot makes two inward swipes at the floor during the turn.

Fouetté En Tournant. A turn in which a whipping motion of the free leg propels the dancer around the supporting leg.

Gesture Leg. The moving leg, opposite to the supporting leg on the floor.

Glissade. A gliding movement from fifth position to an open position and back to fifth position.

GRAND. Large, as in grand jeté, a large jump.

JETÉ. A jump in which the weight of the body is thrown from one foot to the other.

L'AIR. Aloft, as in *tour en l'air*, a turn in the air.

MANÈGE. A circular series of turns; literally, a "merry-go-round."

PAS DE BOURRÉE. A three-step sequence that reverses the positions of the feet from front to back.

PAS DE DEUX. A dance for two people.

PASSÉ. A position in which the toe of the working leg is in contact with the knee of the straight supporting leg. Technically, the term refers to a passing position, but it is often used for a static position as well.

PENCHÉE. Leaning, usually to the front.

PIROUETTE. A complete turn of the body on one foot.

PLIÉ. Lowering of the body by bending the knees.

POINTE. *En pointe* is dancing on the toes.

PROMENADE. A "walk." Usually used to describe a slow turn of the body in place, on one supporting leg, with a constant body position.

QUATRE. Four.

RELEVÉ. The raising of the body onto *pointe* or *demi-pointe*.

RETIRÉ. A standing position in which one foot is at the knee of the supporting leg.

SAUT DE BASQUE. Literally, jump of Basque. A jumping turn carried out while traveling to the side, with take-off from one foot and landing to the other. If traveling to the right, the take-off is from the right foot, the turn is to the right, and the landing is *en face* on the left foot.

SAUTÉ. Jump.

SECOND POSITION. A standing position facing front with the feet spread apart to the side.

SECONDE. Second, as in *à la seconde*, the leg extended to the side in second position.

TOMBÉ. A lunge to the front, side, or back.

TOURNANT. Turning.

TOUR. A turn.

# Glossary of Physics Terms

ACCELERATION.   Rate of change of velocity.

AXIS OF ROTATION.   Line around which a body rotates.

CENTER OF GRAVITY.   Point at which the gravitational force on a body may be considered to act.

FORCE.   The magnitude and direction of "push" or "pull." The total of the forces acting on a body determines its rate of change of momentum.

FORCE COUPLE.   A pair of equal forces acting in opposite directions along parallel lines. A force couple produces a torque on an object with no net force on it.

LINE OF ACTION.   The line along which a force acts, coincident with the direction of the force.

MASS.   The inertial resistance to a change in linear motion. A large mass will accelerate less than a small mass in response to a particular force.

MOMENTUM.   A quantity of motion, equal to the product of the mass and the velocity of a body.

PRECESSION.   The circling of the axis of rotation around the vertical orientation, as a spinning top moves as it slows down.

RESONANCE.   A phenomenon whereby a periodically changing force has the same frequency as a natural frequency of oscillation of a system, allowing the response of the system to the force to grow to a large magnitude. An example is a person pushing a child in a swing, in which the magnitude of the swinging motion grows because the pushing force has the same timing as the natural timing of the oscillating swing.

ROTATIONAL ACCELERATION.   Rate of change of rotational velocity.

ROTATIONAL INERTIA.   The inertial resistance to a change in rotational motion. A body with large rotational inertia will undergo a smaller rotational acceleration in response to a particular torque than a body with small rotational inertia. The rotational inertia depends both on the magnitude of mass of a body and on how that mass is distributed relative to the axis of rotation, with a larger rotational inertia for mass distributed far from the axis.

ROTATIONAL MOMENTUM.   A quantity of rotational motion; the product of the rotational inertia and the rotational velocity.

ROTATIONAL VELOCITY.   Rate of change of rotational orientation.

SPEED.   The magnitude of the velocity, ignoring direction.

TORQUE.   "Turning force." The magnitude of torque determines the rate of change of rotational momentum. A torque arising from a force couple defined above will result in *only* rotational acceleration and no linear acceleration. The magnitude of torque for a force couple consisting of two forces $F$ acting in opposite directions and separated by a distance $D$ is just $F \times D$.

VELOCITY.   Rate of change of position, with magnitude and direction both specified. Velocity and speed are often used interchangeably in everyday speech.

WEIGHT.   The total force of gravity on a body. Mass and weight are often used interchangeably in everyday speech, and in fact are proportional to each other when acted upon by the gravitational force of the earth.

# Index